PROTESTANTS
IN RUSSIA

PROTESTANTS
IN RUSSIA

by
J. A. Hebly
translated by John Pott

William B. Eerdmans Publishing Company

First American edition by Wm. B. Eerdmans Publishing Co.
255 Jefferson Ave. S.E., Grand Rapids, Mich. 49502

Made and Printed in Ireland by
Cahill & Co., Dublin

This book is a translation from the Dutch edition
(1973) of *Protestanten in Rusland*, published by
Uitgeversmaatschappij J. H. Kok N.V., Kampen,
The Netherlands. It appears by permission of Kok.

Library of Congress Cataloging in Publication Data

Hebly, J. A.
    Protestants in Russia.

    Translation of Protestanten in Rusland.
    1.   Protestant churches — Russia.   I.   Title.
BX4849.H413   1975   280′.4′0947   76-149
ISBN 0-8028-1614-2

Contents

Introduction

In the following chapters we want to relate something of the history and life of the Evangelical Christians and Baptists in Russia. From time to time the newspapers publish items about these Christians, and tourists who visit Russia tell of crowded church services they attended in Leningrad and Moscow. Yet generally little is known of them outside Russia. The purpose of this book is to help the interested reader understand the present situation of Evangelical Christians and Baptists in the Soviet Union.

It is not our intention to offer a comprehensive view of the history of the church in old and new Russia. We would then have to concentrate on the Russian Orthodox Church, the national church of old czarist Russia, which today is still by far the largest church in the Union of Soviet Socialist Republics. Compared to this church, the Evangelical Christians and Baptists constitute only a small minority. Yet today they make up the most important group apart from the Orthodox Church. They are extremely vocal, and through their zealous activity and faith are an arresting phenomenon in atheistic Communist society. Their history is both interesting and moving. In czarist times they were violently persecuted, and in the new regime, in different periods, they have lived under heavy oppression. The Evangelical Christian and Baptist movements originated in the second half of the 19th century, so it is only a short period of history with which we are dealing. But before their origin and emergence can be described, we shall have to review something of the history of the church in the preceding centuries.

The old national Russian church forms the background of our subject. Having emerged from it, these movements grew to independence, but in confrontation with the State Church. The danger of absorbing oneself in the history of this long-persecuted minority is that the negative aspects of the czarist-dominated State Church come to be emphasized. This is almost inescapable. We must remember, though, that after the Revolution the national church itself became a persecuted church and was purified through suffering. Through that suffering, the old church of Russia has experienced a renewal in her thinking, especially in regard to a tolerance of the faith of non-Orthodox Christians.

The Orthodox Church of Russia has a thousand-year history behind it, beginning with the conversion of Czar Vladimir of Kiev (987 - 1015) in 988. According to an old chronicle, Vladimir received ambassadors from the most important religions so that they might tell him of their faith. They came from the followers of Islam, from the *chasaren* that followed the Jewish Law, from the Roman Catholics in the West, and from the patriarch of the Greek Orthodox Church in Byzantium. Afterwards he sent out emissaries who were to report their findings to him. These were not happy with the Mohammedan custom of abstaining from pork and wine. (Vladimir commented on this: "The Russians love to drink so much we can't live without it.") The Jewish cult impressed them as joyless and the German was not beautiful enough, but in participating in the Greek Orthodox liturgy they forgot that they were still upon this earth and imagined themselves in heaven. They must have had in mind the service in the

Hagia Sophia in Byzantium (Constantinople), the most important center of Christian culture at that time. An interesting legend : it seems as if the Russians finally chose the Christian faith in its Byzantine form only after a study in comparative religion ! This refers not only to the czar, who after his baptism married the sister of the Byzantine emperor, for by his orders the people were baptized en masse. The Nestorian chronicle has this to say about it : [1]

> All the people gathered by the river upon a sign from Vladimir, threw themselves up to their chest and neck into the water, while holding their children above them. Priests read the baptismal prayers and Vladimir invoked God's blessing upon His new children.

The Christian faith had become the religion of the state in Russia and was to remain so until 1917. The decision of Vladimir to embrace the Orthodox faith and to unite himself with the church of Byzantium had a deep, decisive significance. A schism existed already at that time between the Greek and Latin church, Byzantium and Rome, East and West; there were symptoms even then of a curtain separating two worlds from each other. This separation would be formally established in 1054, when Cardinal Humbert of Rome laid a papal bull of condemnation on the altar in the Hagia Sophia, putting the patriarch of Constantinople under the curse. His response : "God may see and judge." The Russian church has therefore never had any ties with Rome, the center of the Latin church in Western Europe. With its acceptance of the faith in its Greek-Byzantine form it accepted the historic alienation between the Eastern and Western church. The only time a Russian delegate has taken part in an official council was in 1439 in Florence. Metropolitan Isidore of Moscow signed there a reunion decree between Rome and Byzantium, but upon his return to Moscow he was

9

imprisoned by the czar. The Russians considered it a punishment when Constantinople was captured by the Turks in 1453; it would never have happened if they had not left the path of sound religion and sought unity with Rome.

Prior to Vladimir, the Bulgarians under their king Boris (853 - 888) had embraced the Christian faith and recognized the authority of the patriarch of Constantinople. A rich church-Slavic culture arose in Bulgaria and the Cyrillic script was further developed. It was largely through this channel that the young Russian church received the spiritual heritage of Byzantium. The liturgy and the most important ecclesiastical writings were translated into Church Slavonic; to this day it has remained the language in which the liturgy is celebrated. The extension of the Christian life and the Christianizing of the people began under the rule of Vladimir. In our opinion the mass baptisms constituted only a more or less noteworthy beginning. The real spiritual leaders of the people came to be the monks. The first monastery, the famous Caves Monastery, which still exists, was founded in Kiev in 1051 after the pattern of Mt. Athos.

The alienation from Western Europe and its religious development which had already begun with the choice of Constantinople was strengthened by two events. In the beginning of the 13th century, German Catholic knights captured the Baltic countries in the name of a crusade for Christ against the East. Naturally this created much opposition to Western Christendom. Alexander Nevski brought them to a halt, however, in 1242 at Lake Peipus, and Novgorod remained a Russian city. But at the same time disaster of unimaginable proportions struck Russia.

In 1238, quite unexpectedly, the armies of the Mongols (commonly called the Tartars) streamed into Russia from the East. The whole country was conquered and Kiev was reduced to rubble in 1240. The Christians from the West offered no help and even tried to profit from Russia's desperate situation in that dark period. Alexander Nevski had succeeded in repelling the invaders from the West but had to submit to the domination of the Tartars. Russia became occupied country and had to pay tribute, while the Tartars used the Russian princes to govern the country. Their rule, the Kingdom of the Golden Horde, was to last from 1237 to 1480. Dittrich distinguishes two periods here. The direct occupation of the first gave way after 1328 to the second, after the stronger Muscovite princes had gained more important positions and learned how to push back a weakening Tartar influence. Complete independence was finally won in 1480.[2]

The Tartars were tolerant in religious matters and did not touch the church, which was freed from paying tribute and taxes on all its possessions and fields. In those centuries the church was often the only refuge and during that period was very closely involved in the life of the Russian people. The monasteries were carriers and preservers of culture. Many were founded in that time, particularly in the northern territories, where they played an important role in opening up these areas. Famous in this connection is the saintly Sergii of Radonezh (1314 - 1392), founder of the monastery at Zagorsk, today still a spiritual center of orthodoxy and a great tourist attraction.

During this period of Tartar domination the Russian people were strongly isolated from the West. Further separation from Western Europe resulted from the war waged with Roman Catholic Poland and Lithuania, which had occupied vast stretches of Russia. Contact with Constantinople, however, remained. But the actual influence of the declining Byzantine State Church was negligible, and in 1453 Constantinople was conquered by the Turks. Thus ended the Eastern-Roman, Byzantine empire.

In the meantime the Russians, without the co-operation of the patriarch of Constantinople, had elected in Moscow a new metropolitan of Kiev and all Russia. In 1459 the independence of the Russian church was announced at a synod of bishops. The patriarchate of Moscow and all Russia was founded in 1589. A great national consciousness swept over young Moscow, where metropolitan and ruling prince, who received the title of Czar-Caesar, were established in a strong union of throne and altar.

Ivan III (1462 - 1505) was considered a new Emperor Constantine. He refused henceforth to pay taxes to the Golden Horde and adopted the Byzantine double-eagle for his coat of arms. He was considered the successor of the Byzantine emperors, and Moscow was proclaimed the third Rome, replacing the second Rome, Constantinople. The monk Pilotheus wrote : "Two Romes have gone down, but the third one stands, and a fourth shall not arise." Meanwhile the spiritual development of both the people and clerics was extremely low. There were no schools or universities. The priests learned from their fathers what they needed for the practice of their profession; the monasteries also, due to the task of governing their vast possessions, had spiritually declined. Under the influence of the monk Josef of Volokolamsk, reforms were carried through, and a strong conservative current gained the upper hand. Strong measures were taken against anti-trinitarian tendencies which surfaced here and there, the proponents of which were called Judaists. Humanistic tendencies were perceptible in this new thinking, for example, in an attempt to translate anew certain Biblical passages from the Hebrew. But they received no opportunity for further development.

We mention these developments in order to make clear that in Russia the social and spiritual circumstances were totally different from those in Western Europe, where at that time the Reformation was in progress. The spiritual climate of the people was such that a reform movement could not take root there. The Renaissance had had no influence, nor did scholasticism and medieval theology flourish there. There were no humanist Bible scholars in Russia. After all, the reform movement in the Western church had not simply dropped out of the sky but was the result of long development which was also determined by social, economic, and political factors. These were entirely different in Russia. The Reformation, accordingly, has remained a movement within the Latin Church of the West. No Russian Protestant church originated during the time of the Reformation. The 16th-century Reformation came to a halt before the gates of the Orthodox Church, where life was arranged according to old Russian custom. The ordering of home and church life under Metropolitan Makarios (1543 - 1564), during the reign of Ivan IV (the Terrible), was firmly established in the *Domostroi*, a manual in which the rules for everyday life, church attendance, child training, married life, and home life were carefully prescribed.[3] There was no question of any separation between civil and religious life. Not until the time of Peter the Great did Russia open its windows toward the West. Peter introduced social reforms and new rules governing church life. Although strong Protestant influences appeared during that era of openness to the West, there was never any possibility of a reform movement that would give birth to an independent Reformation church.

There was indeed a Lutheran Church in Russia during Peter's reign, because at the time the Baltic countries were being subjugated. For the Reformation at an early date had had great influence in Estonia and Latvia and there existed a mainly German Lutheran Church. The history of this church, however, will remain outside our purview, since it has had no direct influence

13

on the rise of the Evangelical Christians and Baptists.[4] Their existence is rather an outgrowth of the Protestant immigrant church in Russia, the history of which will now engage our attention.

Part I

I. Protestant Immigrants in Russia

If we leave Baltic Protestantism outside our consideration, we can say that at first Protestantism in Russia was a foreign affair. The Protestant congregations of the 16th century originated as a result of individual or group immigration, partly forced as war prisoners were deported from the Baltic countries to Russia. Generally, however, Protestants and also Catholics, but in fewer numbers, came voluntarily to Russia by invitation of Russian princes.

The first Protestant congregations arose not in the country but in the cities. As early as 1576 there was a Lutheran church in Moscow composed principally of Latvian prisoners of war. The minister, Timan Brakel, was taken to Moscow as a hostage along with other outstanding inhabitants of Dorpat after the capture of that city by Czar Ivan IV. As the first Lutheran clergyman in Moscow, he wrote of his stay there:

> So have I also preached the Word of God to others in their homes, as opportunities made it possible, administered the Holy Supper, and when children were born to these Latvian prisoners, I baptized them; further, I visited the

17

> prisoners and comforted the sick, and thus I had
> my church, pulpit, and altar there, no matter
> how difficult and singular things went.[5]

Merchants, artisans, doctors, and military men who came
to Moscow joined themselves to this church. The number
of Germans (the term often used of foreigners regardless
of origin) in Moscow in the year 1602 is estimated to have
been four thousand. A chronicler of this time tells of the
opposition the heretical strangers met from the Orthodox
clergy. Because many Protestants already wore Russian
clothing, they could not be recognized as non-Orthodox
foreigners. It happened that when the patriarch made a
tour through the city, various persons standing along the
way refused to kneel when he gave his blessing. When the
patriarch learned that these were the non-Orthodox
"Germans," he forbade all non-Orthodox to wear Russian
clothing. That created its problems. Someone wrote:

> Therefore each one took what he could first lay
> his hands on: some put on the clothes of their
> parents, grandparents, and great grandparents,
> which at the time of the deportation of the old
> Latvians they had put in boxes and carried along
> to Moscow. This produced great laughter in their
> meetings, not only because these styles were so
> outmoded but also because, for many, these
> clothes were either too big or too small.

The Orthodox Church, up to the time of Peter the
Great, saw to it that social contact with strangers was
limited as much as possible. Rules dated from 1649
stipulated that no one might live under the same roof with
Protestants, or eat with them.[6] In 1652 the czar com-
manded all foreigners, which included many Hollanders
at that time, to live outside the walls of Moscow. There
arose the Sloboda, a district which, as Amburger writes,
resembled a small Dutch or German city, with its own

churches and schools. The Reformed folk also had their church, called the Holland Church, the first minister of which was the Hollander Johannes Bulaeus. Among the ministers of 17th-century Moscow, the German Johann Gottfried Gregorii was undoubtedly the most colorful. He had been a schoolmaster and army chaplain to the first German general in the Russian army and since 1662 a minister in Moscow. Czar Alexis, moreover, had appointed him to superintend theatrical productions at the court. With his pupils and others from his congregation he produced the play *Ahasuerus and Esther*, followed by other pieces similarly edifying. The beginning of a theater school in Moscow!

During the reign of Peter I (the Great) a new influx of migrant workers entered Russia. It is well known how the young Czar Peter was quite at home in the foreign district. He was present at parties and church festivals and was intimately acquainted with various young ladies of Protestant background. Czar Peter powerfully molded the history of his country. He opened the windows to Western Europe and introduced many reforms. A contrast began to appear between the conservatism of old Moscow and the new direction inspired by Western Europe. The anti-Western disposition of the church leaders was one of the important causes of Peter's radical reforms in church government.[7] The patriarchate was abolished and a synodical church government after the German model was introduced so that, in fact, the church was subordinated to the state and the procurator of the czar received decisive new power. Archbishop Feofan Prokopovich, Peter's adviser in ecclesiastical matters, was greatly influenced by Protestantism and especially by the pietism of Halle, which held great interest for the Russians, and he hoped to influence the Russian church in a Protestant direction.

After his journey through Western Europe Peter tried

to get foreign military and technical experts to come to Russia to share his enthusiasm in helping to develop his country. In his manifesto of 1702, he promised them freedom to serve God according to the dictates of their own consciences.[8]

> Seeing that the free exercise of religion has been carried out in our capital city even for those Christian sects which differ with our church, we now reaffirm this policy, and in such a way that we will not abuse the power that the Almighty has given us in bringing pressure of conscience to bear on these people. We leave to every Christian the care for the salvation of his own soul. Accordingly, we will see to it that in harmony with what is customary among us no one will be hindered in his public or private devotions but rather will be protected and defended against all infractions of the law. In case, however, there is no minister or church anywhere within our empire, or in our army, or in any of our garrisons, which is of the same confession, then each one is permitted to hold a religious service not only at home with his family but also with others, in order to praise God according to the general precepts of the Christian church, and thus unitedly engage in a religious service. And if there happen to be in our armies or army-corps, consisting of regiments and companies, Protestant ministers, then, without doubt, these must be accorded the same advantages, privileges, and freedom which we have given their churches here in Moscow, Archangel, and in other places. And this refers not only to a preaching service, but also to the administration of the sacraments, and to other ecclesiastical functions which are in common usage here.

> Moreover, upon the request of those dissidents, we will permit them to build new churches in other places.

He did not, however, permit evangelism among Orthodox believers.

In the new city of St. Petersburg, founded by Peter I along the Neva, there were always many foreign workmen, particularly in the navy. In the middle of the fortress Peter had a little wooden church built for them. The Dutch Admiral Cornelius Cruys who, according to Rev. Dalton, received the title "protector of all the Lutheran and Reformed in the empire," was very active in founding Protestant congregations in St. Petersburg. Through the founding of an academy in 1725, in which many foreigners were involved, many intellectuals joined the Protestant population. Among the church members one finds also the names of Baltic noblemen who were at the court. Thus the St. Petersburg congregations experienced great growth. The spiritual condition, however, did not differ much from that in other parts of Europe during that time. The Enlightenment permeated the thinking, and had as elsewhere very little stimulating effect on spiritual growth in the life of these churches. The Orthodox environment remained untouched by them. The various big-city congregations reflected a bourgeois-aristocratic character and led a fairly isolated existence. The Dutch congregation, of which we shall write below, is an example of this. The Protestant congregations, united as they were since 1832 in an ecclesiastical confederation, yet had very little direct contact with each other. The majority of Protestant immigrants—more than 90 per cent—lived in the colonies in the south. Protestant church life in St. Petersburg, which soon after the founding of the city far surpassed in importance that in Moscow, nevertheless represented only a small part of the Protestant church in Russia. Yet due to the social relationships existing particularly among the elite, there was some indirect influence upon the Orthodox milieu. Lutheran noblemen from the Baltic countries, for example, often filled high positions at the court. These contacts in St. Petersburg, during the second half of the 19th century, prepared the soil for the growth of an evangelical movement among the Russians themselves.

During the 18th century and the beginning of the 19th, many agricultural colonies arose in the south. A large number of foreigners during the reign of Catherine II (1762 - 1796) were attracted to Russia to settle those areas which had been so largely depopulated as a result of the Russian - Turkish Wars. Russian farmers were unavailable for this purpose due to the serfdom which prevented their mobility. Foreigners were recruited with the promise of religious liberty and exemption from military service and from taxation for thirty years. Germans especially left for Russia, and along the Volga between the years 1764 and 1767 some 104 colonies were founded. The oppression suffered by the Mennonites in Lutheran Prussia led them also to emigrate after they heard of Catherine's manifesto. After 1789 many of them settled along the lower region of the Dnieper and in other districts in southern Russia. Migrating within the empire, they spread into West Siberia. They too were exempted from military service as well as from swearing an oath, immunities which Czar Nicholas I renewed. In 1874 when the exemption from military service was annulled for the colonists, a number of them emigrated to North America and Canada. The authorities responded by offering the Mennonites the opportunity for substitute service. In 1805-1809 and 1813 - 1817 a number of farm families came to Russia from the West. Despite help from the Russian authorities, the first years were particularly difficult for the colonists. H. Dalton, the well-known Reformed minister from St. Petersburg, who knew the life of these

22

congregations firsthand, wrote about them as follows:

> The grandfathers in the colonies still tell us how in the beginning they dug holes in the ground. They would dig a large, square, deep hole which would then be covered with branches, reeds, and earth. On the inside, everything was smeared with mud. There they spent the first winter. But already the following year four strong corner posts were sunk into the ground on which were laid crossbeams with rafters; the crossbeams were covered with thin branches, and the branches with reeds and shrubs; the space up to the rafters was filled in with branches woven together, and the whole was smeared inside and out with mud. Thus they began already to live a little better. And now things have improved much more. The traveler strikes it lucky when in the summer he has covered a few miles through the burning, treeless steppe in a none-too-comfortable wagon, and then, toward evening, rides into a friendly colony along the highway. The houses have been neatly built, brick by brick, all arranged the same way. If you enter the house from the street, coming through the garden, the kitchen lies straight ahead, while the living room is on your left and the bedroom on your right. The guest generally gets the bedroom where one is struck by the clean bed and the high-piled cushions. The living room is clean but furnished very plainly, with sitting benches generally of unfinished wood. In the corner on a little shelf are a few books of spiritual content.[9]

In the first quarter of the 19th century a large wave of immigrants, principally from Baden, Württemberg, and Bavaria, but also from Switzerland, entered Russia. Forced to seek their livelihood elsewhere because of the

23

depressed economic conditions following the Napoleonic Wars, they were further motivated by religious considerations to seek their fortunes in the land of Czar Alexander I (1801 - 1825). The czar, regarded as a messianic figure by many Germanic people influenced by religious revival, could well benefit from the help of these immigrants in rebuilding his land. A craftsman from Einenden wrote :

> What induced me to leave with my family—my wife and nine healthy children—was the high cost of living in the year 1817. Yet even more important was a strong desire to live in a country ruled by a humane emperor, where many godly noblemen were concerned about the temporal and eternal welfare of the inhabitants.[10]

In the politically unstable and confused times around the turn of the century, many pious folk looked for the coming of Christ. Johann Heinrich Jung-Stilling, writer and physician, exerted great influence in certain religious circles. Particularly in his two books *Heimweh* (1794) and *Sieges-Geschichte der Christlichen Religion* (1799) he had developed the idea that the Antichrist was at hand, soon to destroy the work of Christ. He saw its unmistakable signs both in political developments and in the spiritual decline of the church, brought on by rationalistic theology. All churches were seduced by the spirit of Antichrist; the duty of true Christians was to try to revive the spirit of true Christianity in these churches. If this endeavor should fail, they must unite and travel to the East. There the true congregation of Jesus would find a refuge (Rev. 12), an ark of safety in the fearsome days of the end-time, and there the Kingdom of God would be built. He calculated that this would occur in 1826. His ideas took hold, and were spread, among others, by Baroness de Krüdener. And so the devout multitudes journeyed eastward to Odessa and as far as the Sea of Azov, where different groups settled. One band pressed even further, deep into the Caucasus, to find safety and happiness. When in the year 1818 a group entered the valley of Tiflis, one of their wagons carried the banner : "Here comes the multitude of the faithful." They received the land granted them, and here they settled next to each other as they had lived in their former homeland, with relatives or fellow villagers. For more than a hundred years they were to remain here, until the horrors of another war drove them on.

Their spiritual background gave these congregations a distinctive character. Some formed exclusive congregations which found it most difficult to unite with the Evangelical Lutheran Church of Russia. Time and again revival broke out among these congregations which, through language and religion, were quite isolated in this Russian Orthodox country. They did exert an influence on other German congregations. Revival preachers with their call to conversion and new life wielded a strong influence, and the mission program carried on in the Caucasus by Basel since 1821 also contributed to this cause. "Thus the spiritual history of these congregations was largely one of revivals," writes W. Kahle.[11] Dalton[12] writes of it in these words:

> The environment, isolation from the world, the spirit which withdraws within itself, the loneliness—all have developed to a high degree an exclusive religious life one finds in few places. The colonist lives solely by the language of the Bible, and it is his greatest joy to busy himself with it and the catechism. Morning and evening prayers in which the whole family shares has become a fixed custom. From the old fatherland Württemberg they kept the practice of devotional hours almost everywhere clung to except by the lowest strata in the community which no longer adheres to the old ways. With moving patience

25

the conversation in these hours confines itself year after year within the narrow limits of fixed beloved religious concepts. These folk are very liberal when it comes to missions, often running into some ten thousand francs which, for example, Basel receives from these forgotten and lonely villages.

Notwithstanding the stirring and attractive aspects, one may not overlook the negative side. As in some areas the Word of God is precious, so there are also areas where it has become cheap. A fervent and devout pietistic current must carefully guard against the great danger of being too onesidedly attentive to the religious while paying too little attention to ethical requirements. Actually, one cannot separate the one from the other, but a onesided preoccupation with the one leads to a caricature of both. From the happy awareness of having been saved by grace through Jesus Christ, an even happier consciousness must follow that from the same abundance of grace one must grow in sanctification into the complete man. And this is forgotten in many places in the colonies. Thus in many conversations one distinguishes sharply between the converted and unconverted, whereas no difference in lifestyle is to be noted on both sides.

The German colonists were greatly influenced by two leaders, Johann Bonekemper (1796 - 1854) and Eduard Wüst (1818 - 1859). Bonekemper, born on the Rhine, was trained at the mission school in Basel. In 1824 he went to Russia at the invitation of Ignaz Lindl, who sought young men who "by a heartfelt penitence and living faith had come to love Christ and were prepared to go there." He became the leader of congregations in Rohrbach and Worms in the Ukraine (twelve miles from Odessa), consisting largely of Reformed folk who had come from the Palatinate and Württemberg and organized in 1809. He remained there twenty-four years, laboring with great blessing and exerting a positive influence in the surrounding area. In those spiritually neglected congregations his Bible lectures grew into *Bibelstunden* — pietist-flavored meetings introduced by song and prayer, where the Bible was read and explained. The emphasis was on a fervent spiritual life, personal regeneration, and an aversion to the evil world. Somewhat less influential was the preaching of E. Wüst who, because of his separatist-pietist tendencies in Germany, was deposed from his office and in 1845 came to Berdikhev near the Sea of Azov. All sorts of ecstatic and libertine excesses took place particularly after his death in 1859. His influence was noticeable among both the Catholic and Mennonite colonies. Although he zealously worked to have a congregation of those truly born again, Christians assured of their faith, and permitted only twice-born Christians to partake of the Lord's Supper, yet he did not introduce adult baptism. Various Mennonite congregations, however, did; while they naturally knew about adult baptism, certain groups now determined upon baptism by immersion. Through these groups came contacts with German Baptists. Johann Gerhard Oncken (1800 - 1884), called the father of the German Baptist movement, established further contact with Stundism in the German colonies when in 1869 he arrived in the Ukraine. Independent Baptist congregations arose in Old and New Danzig in the neighborhood of modern Kirovograd.

The developments in the Protestant colonies of south Russia described here are not uncharacteristic of Russian Protestantism in general. Spiritual development elsewhere was generally even, though still somewhat isolated, of course, from the development in Western Europe. A peaceful and orderly congregational life was maintained, complete with school and church, pastors, and the not-to-be-forgotten school sextons who were also often burdened with religious instruction. In the city congregations, such as in St. Petersburg and Moscow, the character of life differed from that in the Lutheran Baltic provinces or in the self-contained farming settlements. All of them, however, were united in an ecclesiastical union and came under the ruling of the "law for Evangelical Lutheran Churches in Russia," signed on December 28, 1832, by the czar. Subject to this church order built on strict Lutheran principles, Russian Protestantism was to live for eighty-five years. European and Asiatic Russia each had its own district with its own government. The church order was imposed from above, and this government regulation seriously impeded individual church initiative and self-government. The church was governed by consistories the members of which were state appointed. Thus the state government had great influence. The Reformed folk were also included in this church union, even though a separate committee administered their affairs. Dalton[13] tells us that for many it was difficult to accept this new regulation.

> Thus the congregations lived peacefully until the year 1833. It was the time when a new Lutheran church order was being completed in St. Petersburg. In developing this new project particular attention was paid to the Baltic provinces, where a homogenous Lutheran population had preserved its old traditions. Incomprehensibly, however, the writers had failed to reckon with the particular needs of more than 200,000 colonists who in the church of their fatherland had never known the strict Lutheran liturgy with its more fully developed altar service, and the more than 40,000 Reformed folk who knew nothing of an altar service and crucifixes and burning candles

in broad daylight. Nor did they know about prayers sung by the minister while his back was turned to the congregation. Everywhere almost without exception, the introduction of this new "order" caused excitement in the south. As a case in point, Lutheran Württembergers refused to have burning candles on the altar and to hear their ministers sing the prayers. Concessions, therefore, had to be made which are still in force.

The only seminary in the Russian empire, the German faculty of Dorpat, organized in 1802 for Protestant theologians, exercised great theological influence. A number of theologians trained there found their way to the colonial congregations. More ministers came from Germany and Switzerland, as occurred in the 18th century. But there was a continual dearth of leaders in the rural congregations which, left to themselves, had to be satisfied with reading services or with sermons delivered by fellow brethren. The importance of the role played by these preaching brethren was second only to that of the traditional pastors. Later on, when they had to depend even more upon their own resources, this would prove a great blessing. Barring the congregations in the Volga district, where the colonists lived together in a self-contained community, the areas served by each preacher were often very extensive. The largest parish in the Russian empire was Irkutsk, where one minister had the pastoral care of a territory many times larger, than the Netherlands. Through migrations of the colonists within the empire and through deportations, a number of congregations sprang up in Siberia as well, where, due to ecclesiastical pressure on the government. Protestant exiles were assigned to one district. In 1819 the first in a series of exile congregations was founded in West Siberia. In such areas, however, the minister could hardly keep contact with his church members. The most he could do was attend to some official duties, especially conducting weddings, a task entrusted to him by the state when Protestants were involved. But this also created problems, as a German doctor experienced. He had to wait two years before a minister arrived to wed him to his Finnish bride. Because they wanted to give their children a Protestant education, they refused to have an Orthodox priest perform the ceremony.

In daily life there was little contact between the members of the different confessions. Partly because of their foreign descent and language, but also because of their confession, the Protestant congregations in Russia lived in spiritual isolation. The co-operation fostered by the Bible Society, which developed under Alexander I, was only an interlude during which Orthodoxy was intensively exposed to the influence of certain Protestant currents. Naturally, the Protestants constituted only a minority. Prior to the First World War the number of Germans in the Volga territory was estimated at 700,000; in southern Russia and the Caucasus, 600,000.[14]

Toleration of foreigners, a consequence of the need for foreign advisers and workmen, continued up to the First World War, and stands out favorably above many Western European countries. The manifesto issued by Catherine the Great on July 22, 1763, regulated the religious and ecclesiastical rights of the immigrants and remained in effect until the Toleration Act of 1905. By that act, permission was granted to choose one's own confession, as well as to exercise the right to leave the Orthodox Church for another faith. Up to that time it was forbidden for any Russian Orthodox believer to transfer his membership to the Evangelical Lutheran Church. In the instructions for ministers[15] it was clearly forbidden to tempt any Orthodox Christian by word or any other means to transfer to another communion. Even a request from members of another church for doctrinal instruction and eventual membership in the church was to be refused. Severe punishments were prescribed for those who did not adhere to the rule. Transference of membership to the Orthodox State Church, however, was open to everyone, and might not be hindered in any way. Moreover, ministers were forbidden to solemnize mixed marriages and to baptize children born of such marriages.

The Protestants in the Russian empire were as strangers pressed into a spiritual isolation, and every manifestation of missionary fervor was repressed by law. That, nonetheless, sparks from a fervent life of faith were able to blow over to Russian believers out of these isolated congregations and that eventually these developed into forms of Russian Protestantism is all the more remarkable. Especially those Protestant communions with a pietist orientation and an eschatologically-determined life of faith were a formidable influence on those around them.

II. The Dutch in Russia

In the village of Vriezenveen in the district of Twente, Holland, there is a museum which includes a Russian section in which are preserved all sorts of mementos reminding us of the merchants of Vriezenveen who, from the beginning of the 18th century, carried on business with St. Petersburg. In a Lübeck saloon, according to a popular legend, a merchant from Vriezenveen met a Norse seaman who told him that there was big money to be earned in Russia and offered him free passage there. He did a thriving business in St. Petersburg, just recently founded by Peter the Great, and back in his native village succeeded in getting others interested. Contact between Vriezenveen and St. Petersburg was established. Leaving Lübeck by ship, or moving overland in covered wagons, these enterprising Hollanders went to Russia and eventually established their commercial houses. They were called the *Rusluie*.[16]

After a chapter on Protestant immigrant churches, we must tell you something of the Dutchmen in Russia. Not that they had any influence on the origin of Protestant currents in Russia, but because their story is a necessary complement to the history of the immigrant churches, and to show that in earlier times Russia was much closer to many Hollanders than is the case today. When we read of "German" immigrants in Russia, this often refers to a much more varied group than the use of the name "German" would suggest. Except for the Mennonites, religious considerations played no role among the Dutch immigrants. They were, quite frankly, interested only in making a living. When the emperor Ivan "the Terrible" began to seek contact with Western Europe, the Hollanders were immediately ready to carry on business and—to borrow a modern phrase—to make a contribution to progress. J. Scheltema[17] mentions a letter written by Ivan to Charles V in which he requests scholars, artists, architects, manufacturers, and tradesmen, and also

> theologians, in order that they, being called and accepted in this country, may become thoroughly versed in our language, religion, and ceremonies; and that we, on the other hand, may be instructed in the faith and confession of the Latin churches and thus may differ less if at some time a council or general synod is convened.

Of this early ecumenical attempt nothing then was realized, but during the reign of Ivan Dutch tradesmen did indeed go to Moscow, and the first commercial houses were established in Moscow, Archangel, and other cities. In 1553 the Englishman Richard Chancellor had reached the northern coasts of Russia by way of the White Sea, and thus the Englishmen were able to gain business concessions with Moscow. The Dutch merchants seemed to have gained the same concessions in 1555. In 1584 near the monastery of the archangel Michael, the wooden city of Archangel was built, and the Hollanders were among the first inhabitants. But Archangel functioned as a trade city for only a short period of the year. The chief merchants spent the winter in Moscow and carried on business from there. Others remained in Archangel, where there was also a Dutch church. Hollanders had also settled in other cities. Scheltema[18] writes :

33

If there were a hundred Hollanders in 1637 in Nizhni Novgorod on the Volga, how many must there have been in the more northern districts of the empire, in Vologda, Ustivg, and Yaroslavl, because the trade in goods carried on in those areas formed a much larger part of the total business than that carried on in the southern territories.

But the most important establishment was in Moscow, where church life also found its center. Mention is made of a Reformed Church in Moscow already in 1616, but how much longer it had already existed cannot be determined. Books and registers were destroyed in the great fires of 1737 and 1812, when Reformed church buildings were completely devastated.[19] Nor do the municipal archives of Moscow reveal anything about the church during that period.[20] In the new foreign quarter, the *Sloboda* (*novaya inosemskaya sloboda*), the Reformed folk built a wooden church called the Holland Church. In 1684 a stone church was built with help from the Netherlands. General Lefort, the famous teacher and adviser of Peter the Great, added a belfry to it. The first ministers of this congregation to be mentioned are Johannes Bulaeus (1629 - 1648), Johannes Kraaywinkel (1650 - 1677), called from Archangel, and Theodorus Schoonrewoerd (1680 - 1704), well known for his learning. The congregation's most flourishing period was near the end of the 17th century. There were then so many Hollanders in Moscow that a second minister was called. Reformed folk from other nationalities belonged to the church, and even Catholics, who had neither church nor priest of their own in Moscow at that time, came to church there. The fact that a minister was called from Archangel suggests that there were ministers there already before the fire of 1667. Scheltema[21] says : "Regarding either the period of their service or of their fate, no notation can be found. The

34

new church was built there in 1674." But the name of Reverend Willem Coster, called there in 1660, is mentioned. The Reformed and Lutheran congregations in Archangel were united in 1817. But by that time the Reformed congregation had become completely German-speaking. In Nizhni Novgorod the Reformed Dutch congregation had already fallen into decay in 1664.

At the end of the first volume of his work on Russia and the Netherlands, the work dealing with the period from Ivan through the death of Fedor in 1682, Scheltema observes :

> From all this we confidently draw the conclusion that the nation of Holland was the best known in Russia, and also the most loved during the childhood and youth of Czar Alexis' youngest son Peter.

Under Czar Peter we see the Reformed congregation in Moscow slowly deteriorating. During that time many left for St. Petersburg, the new city whose growth Peter promoted in as many ways as possible. In 1718 one minister was still left in Moscow. The last minister mentioned was Willem Theodorus van Sandhagen from Zutphen who served during the years 1724 - 1740. He witnessed the departure of a large number of his prosperous church members to the new Dutch congregation in St. Petersburg. After him no more sermons were preached in the Dutch language. The name "Holland Church" remained, however, even in 1860 when the Dutch Reformed congregation in St. Petersburg offered to give financial assistance for the building of a Reformed parsonage. A flourishing Reformed church had arisen in St. Petersburg soon after the founding of the city. The first worship services were held in the house chapel of the famous admiral Cornelius Cruys. Cruys had been rear admiral and boatswain with the admiralty in Amsterdam. When Czar Peter visited the Netherlands in 1697 - 1698, he persuaded Cruys to allow him to accompany him back to Russia. There he became one of the czar's chief collaborators. It was he who, as Scheltema put it,[22] "brought Russian sea power to completion, from the shipyard to the water." But Cruys made himself useful not only to the Russian navy. He was also the organizer of the first Evangelical Lutheran congregation in St. Petersburg. Since his mother was Norse, Cruys was Lutheran and had built a Lutheran chapel near his home. But he was also concerned about his Reformed countrymen and saw to it that a minister from the Netherlands was sent to them. In 1704, after Cruys had visited Holland, another 500 went. At that time Cruys also took with him a Lutheran minister, Willem Tolle. Worship services were held in a wooden chapel in the garden of his home. Instead of a bell to announce the beginning of a service, a white flag with a blue cross was hoisted. In 1717 the Dutch Reformed congregation was organized and the Classis of Amsterdam was asked to send a minister.[23]

The Rev. Mr. Hermannus Grube was the first in a succession of ministers to serve this congregation. The list of St. Petersburg ministers was completed by Dr. H. P. Schim van de Loeff who, after the Revolution of 1920, was forced to leave the country. The money for the support of church and minister—in 1730 a small school building was rearranged to serve as a church, which in 1743 was replaced by the first brick church—was gathered through voluntary gifts and ship levies. Every ship entering the harbor of Kronstadt or St. Petersburg under the Dutch flag paid five rubles for the support of the church. This practice led to problems in 1850, when Catholic shippers refused to pay for the Reformed church service. They were told, however, that these funds had long been used exclusively to help seamen and the poor. The congregation at that time had grown very prosperous. A Dutch schoolmaster was appointed and an organist belonged to the church staff. We do not intend to fully recount the various experiences of the church. Congregational life continued without any major upheavals. In the 19th century, many immigrants from Vriezenveen settled there and amassed large stores and commercial houses. They achieved much success not only in the textile business but in other fields as well. The carpenter's apprentice, Wicher Berkhof, advanced to the position of admiral and chief of the navy wharfs. In 1834 a beautiful new church was dedicated on the Nevsky Prospekt, the large boulevard in St. Petersburg. The building stood in the middle of large Dutch commercial houses and stands to the present day, a library being housed there now. In 1831 when the first stone was laid, the local minister, the Rev. Mr. E. A. J. Tamling, said :

> Here a friendly house of prayer will rise for us, dedicated to God and our Savior. A house in which we and our children and our descendants will hear the voice of God, and out of His Holy Word draw courage and strength and comfort in the storms and changes of life. Here, about this holy place, buildings will rise, destined to be springs and streams which will spread happiness and contentment, wiping away the tears of sorrow, and driving away and lifting from us cares, dangers, and anxieties.

His reference was to the church homes (*kerkehuizen*) that reflected the wealth of the congregation, the earnings of which were used for charitable causes. This Rev. Tamling, minister in St. Petersburg from 1819 to 1842,[24] wrote a number of letters to his teacher and fatherly friend L. Suringar in Leiden, in which is presented an interesting commentary on the spiritual situation in Russia during the reign of Alexander I and his successor, Nicholas I. He writes of the influence the Enlightenment had upon Baltic Lutheranism and upon Protestantism in the rest of

Russia. He tells us, for example, that in 1803 a projected church order for the Lutherans was worded thus: "The Protestant Church has as its sole objective helping members achieve the highest goal for man, mortality and contentment, considering the religious needs of the congregation with the guidance of Reason." He also knew of the reaction of Pietism to this emaciated religiosity of the modernists of that era. Shortly after his arrival an imperial edict was issued, protecting the Evangelical churches from unchristian novelties. The pietist prince Golitsin, Alexander's secretary of state, found "the present ministers to be even more cunning than the Jesuits, all neologists." Tamling helped prepare the new church regulation for the Evangelical churches in Russia and provided explanatory notes. He tried to focus the state committee members' attention on the confession and order of the Reformed Church of his fatherland. "In Holland we stay far away from fickleness and the neglect of evangelical truths and thus keep safe from mysticism with all its dangers." He was not much taken in by the prevailing pietist current. The chairman of the state committee on church affairs told him, "I was also saved through God's grace some four years ago. It would please me if you could call a prayer meeting in your home to speak of God and His service." "I understood what he meant," writes Tamling. "The Moravian Brethren have such meetings where the chairman, vice chairman, even A. (Czar Alexander) himself secretly appear; so I said to him, 'In Holland each family is free to hold such meetings but for everyone to double religious activities is not recommended'." Because of his reactionary politics, he did not admire Prince Golitsin, whom he called "a raving admirer of the mystique." According to him, the prince "was absolutely not the godly man he was considered outside of Russia." He spoke also of the remarkable Baroness de Krüdener, who had such great influence on the czar with her millennial dreams and who "also spouts forth her pious exaggerations here." Tamling states that she once said to a young merchant : "Nature is beautiful, but even more so for him who enjoys God's grace. You, my friend, are still sunk deep in the mire, but the deeper you are sunk, the higher, by grace, you can rise." "Madame said this," writes Tamling, "perhaps with reference to herself, and for her own comfort at the remembrance of former days." He had met one of her followers, "completely ecstatic," who had claimed that "the devils crept up and down my back, but I spat them out in the name of Jesus." "A sad state of affairs here," he lamented. "Fanaticism equals piety, people openly champion the Catholics, the Moravians are much loved." He also complains of the Lutherans who "galloped" all over to hear J. E. Gossner, who was preaching in St. Petersburg in those days.

Tamling reflected the state of mind of many ministers who were quite blind to the new spiritual currents. They saw only the dark shadows of narrow-mindedness and exaggeration, and criticized from a facile acceptance of their own parochial position. Tamling's letters are remarkable for their silence about the Orthodox Church. He seems to have had very few relations with the Orthodox clergy. A peace-loving middle-of-the-roader, he was most satisfied with his congregation. He did complain that it was almost impossible to import books due to the censorship imposed by Czar Nicholas. Through private contacts, however, he knew how to lay his hands on some. The Dutch members of his congregation came to church faithfully, the German members a little less. Six years after his arrival, his congregation consisted of 160 members, of whom 130 were members in full standing. As to the Reformed, he wrote in 1828, "Everything is in good order, the fewest complaints come from them, and also the fewest divorces, and for the rest, everything is quiet and well in the life of the congregation; no fanatical divisiveness is in control here, no separatists impose their private views on others. Ideas that make for peace are the uppermost." A bit of Reformed self-satisfaction seems not to be alien to our minister !

The Tradesmen's Church in St. Petersburg, officially part of the Reformed jurisdiction of the Evangelical Lutheran Consistory of St. Petersburg, was dissociated from the Evangelical Church in 1842 and was recognized as an Embassy Church. Czar Nicholas' decision that every minister in Russia must swear allegiance to the czar and become a Russian citizen made it difficult to attract a minister from the Netherlands. The Rev. Mr. W. L. Welter, who succeeded Tamling (1842 - 1867), was the first to come under the special protection of the embassy. The special place of the Dutch congregation within Russian Protestantism is hereby clearly shown. The congregation never became a connecting link between Protestantism in the Netherlands and Russian Orthodoxy; not much influence was exerted either upon the Netherlands or Russia. With the departure of the Netherland Colony, Dutch church life disappeared in Russia after the Revolution. The influence upon Russian spiritual life came from those immigrants whose coming to Russia was more clearly religiously motivated. Naturally, hidden channels connect Dutch immigration with the Russian Protestants of today. In 1927 Th. Meyer,[25] on a trip through Siberia, met a small Russian-speaking congregation in the neighborhood of Irkutsk. They told him they were *Golendri*—descendants from Hollanders who lived in Russia during the time of Peter the Great. Doubtless there were others who, settling among the Russian people, finally merged with the Evangelical Christians and Baptists. Their history, however, is beyond our present concern.

III. The Russian Bible Society in the Time of Alexander I

The Baroness Julie de Krüdener (1764 - 1824) played a remarkable role in the life of Czar Alexander I.[26] She was born in Riga, a daughter of the German-Baltic family of Von Wietinghoff. The Moravian Brethren had acquired considerable influence in Latvia. In reaction to the stiff dogmatism of 17th-century Lutheranism, they preached a warm personal faith. The baroness had encountered them in her youth, but it was not until later that she experienced her personal conversion. When she was eighteen she married the much older Baron de Krüdener, Russian ambassador in Venice and later in Copenhagen. Unhappy in her marriage, she led a frivolous and restless life, from time to time reuniting with her husband, whom she left permanently in 1801. She spent much of her time in Geneva and Paris, where she survived the capture of the Bastille and where, in 1803, she published her book, *Valerie*.[27] It was the time when Romanticism was beginning, the time of sensitivity, tears, tombstones, loneliness, and passion. Napoleon wanted no part of *Valerie*, of which he said : "Give this foolish baroness my personal advice henceforth to write her books in Russian or in German, that we may be spared this intolerable literature." This not altogether unjust remark turned her into a fiery antagonist.

In 1804 she returned to Riga where, one day, some-one passing her window and greeting her suffered a heart attack and fell dead to the pavement. For her this was a moment of inner collapse. A shoe cobbler introduced the deeply shocked baroness to a group of Moravian Brethren, among whom she found comfort and learned to know her Savior and Lord. To a friend she wrote: "You have no idea what happiness this sublime and holy religion gives me." Then came more travel. In southern Germany she came in contact with millennial currents of thought and met Jung-Stilling. She was captivated by the idea of the imminence of God's Kingdom. A group, a conventicle, gathered around her, sharing her preoccupation with the prophecies of the end-time. She saw Napoleon as the fore-runner of the Antichrist, Alexander of Russia as the great eagle (Rev. 12) who would gather and lead the rescued. She sent her prophecies to him and longed to meet him.

The tragedy that struck his country—defeat at the hands of Napoleon, the fire of Moscow—had been for Czar Alexander a deep religious experience. Daily he read in his French pocket Bible, and on the evening of his departure for the army to launch the pursuit of the French troops, December 6, 1812, he gave permission for the formation of a Russian Bible Society, which was to supervise the translation and distribution of the Bible in his country. Later, in Berlin, he said to a German bishop: "The fire of Moscow has enlightened my soul, and the judgments of the Lord on the frozen steppes have filled my heart as never before with a deep-felt religious warmth." In 1814 he met Jung-Stilling, who urged him to give guidance to the rescue of the faithful in the stirring times that were coming. In 1815, enroute to Vienna, he spoke with Baroness de Krüdener in Heilbronn. The first conversation lasted three hours. The czar entered the following excerpt of the conversation in his diary:

No, Sire, you have not yet approached the God-

Man as a criminal who comes to sue for mercy, you have not yet received mercy from Him who alone has the authority to forgive sins upon the earth. You are yet in your sin, you have not yet humbled yourself before Jesus, you have not yet cried out as the publican from the depths of your heart : "O God, have mercy upon me, a gross sinner." And that is why you still have no peace. Listen to the voice of a woman who was also a gross sinner, but who received the forgiveness of her sins at the foot of the cross of Christ.

She saw in him the savior of the world and impressed upon him that he was the chosen instrument of God. Alexander was not insensitive to these ideas. After he heard the news of the victory at Waterloo, he sank to his knees and prayed :

How happy I am that my savior is with me ! Gross sinner that I am, He wants to use me to bring peace to the nations. O, if only all peoples desired to understand the ways of Providence, how happy we would be.

Alexander and Madame de Krüdener were staying in Paris at the time. She conducted a religious drawing room with prayers and political-religious conversations. Many contemporaries saw her as the inspirer of the Holy Alliance (Dan. 11: 30), the covenant between the rulers of Austria, Prussia, and Russia, based on "the high truths contained in the eternal religion of Christ, our Savior." After 1816 our baroness devoted herself to the work of evangelism, forsaking the drawing rooms to reach out to the thousands. Notwithstanding continual harassment by the police in Switzerland and Austria, she continued to propagandize in favor of emigration to Russia. Her son-in-law served as agent for the pious emigrants who, in the care of the czar, would wait for the coming of the Kingdom of God. Finally she retired to her estate in Latvia. She died on a trip in southern Russia in '1824 and was buried in the Crimea.

We are not here concerned with such personal history, however interesting, from the beginning of the 19th century. To be sure, it does give us a picture of the spiritual climate in which Czar Alexander lived, and of that remarkable episode in the history of Russia when, under czarist direction, the work of Bible distribution in Russia began. On January 11, 1813, the official opening session of the Bible Society took place.[28]

> It was a brilliant meeting that took place in the spacious rooms of the Tauric palace in St. Petersburg. Never before had one seen the highest dignitaries of state and church so united and inspired in faith, embark on so great a task. It seemed as if in that moment those 40 assembled men had laid aside the garments of their confessions, and had put on the honorable robe which alone assures us of the name of Christ. A word spoken that day by a Russian bishop to an Evangelical missionary when they shook hands had profound meaning. The Russian knows the proverb : 'When it thunders, the farmer crosses himself.' "Well, we have heard God's thunder," he said, by which he meant the invasion of Napoleon, "and this now is the Russian people crossing themselves."

The Bible Society in St. Petersburg became the meeting place of Orthodox and Lutherans, Catholics and Reformed. The laity played an important role, among them, Prince Lieven, from a pietistically-disposed Baltic Lutheran family, and Prince Golitsin, Alexander's secretary of state. Among the members, however, were also metropolitans of the Orthodox Church. The work of

Bible translation and distribution went forward with great zeal. Sunday schools were organized, and prisoners were given Bibles. Metropolitan Philaret was the first chairman of the committee whose task it was to translate the Bible into Russian. Up to that time people had access only to the Church Slavonic Bible, which was difficult to understand. Parts of the New Testament in Russian and Slavic were first to appear. In 1823 permission for an edition of a Russian New Testament was given; its distribution was the concern of 300 chapters spread over the whole land.[29] Other religious writings from Protestant-Pietist background were also translated.

Prince Alexander Golitsin was the first chairman of the Bible Society; it was he, after all, who had proposed its founding to the czar. As procurator for the Orthodox State Church, he was entrusted with guiding the Committee on Foreign Confessions which the czar had instituted. All this greatly offended the conservative Orthodox folk who felt that their church was being put on the same level with those who believed otherwise, thereby suffering loss of its dignity. Golitsin maintained close contact with the revival movement and tried to recruit Catholic and Protestant clerics for Russia.[30] He wrote a friend in Bavaria : "We need good priests for all kinds of churches." In 1819 Ignaz Lindl came to Russia to serve as a priest in the Catholic Maltese Church, to be followed a year later by his friend Johannes Gossner; they both belonged to the revival movement in Bavaria. They considered the historic confessions as the many-sided earthly shape in which the true church of Christ hides itself. It was this true church they wanted to serve. They were received with open arms. Gossner wrote after his arrival : [31] "As cold as the climate here, as warm are the hearts." Laboring in St. Petersburg from 1820 to 1823, he filled the churches. The Orthodox of St. Petersburg who understood German joined the Lutherans and the Reformed in attending church to hear this Catholic priest. He also held prayer meetings in the homes. Lindl went to Odessa and established a colony in Bessarabia that expanded into a spiritual center for the whole district. The Basel Mission received permission to begin its work in the area of the Caucasus. Eastern and Western Christendom seemed to join in a supra-confessional union, the rallying point of which was the mystical-spiritual experience of being laid hold on by the Spirit of Christ. Mystical writings, among others those of Jung-Stilling, were translated into Russian and gained wide distribution. An influential priest from the Nevski convent translated Gossner's writing, *The Blessedness Of The Christian In Whose Heart Jesus Dwells*.

But there was also opposition, as we have already seen in our Dutch minister. Other Protestant ministers, too, looked upon the work of Gossner with a certain suspicion. They objected to a preacher who attracted church members to himself, and they did not agree with his ideas. The strongest objections, however, came from the circle of the traditional clergy. Ludolf Müller[32] says that the Protestant influence grew so strong that a reaction was inevitable. The representatives of the old, strict Orthodoxy were not without reason in fearing that the wave of Protestant spiritualism and biblicism would inundate Orthodoxy, and that the church fathers would be crowded out by the Protestant mystics and pietists. In some Western European circles there were those who dreamed of a new Reformation in Russia. A speaker at a meeting of the British Bible Society is supposed to have said that the Society would reveal to the Russian church her errors, revive her faith, and soon bring about a Reformation in Russia.[33] Dispersed among the Orthodox clergy, these words stirred up increased opposition to the work of the Bible Society. The strongest opposition came from the archimandrite Foti from the St. George convent near Novgorod, a man who, according to Pushkin, was half fanatic and half deceiver : "His spiritual weapons are cross and club, curse and sword. Lord, send us as few as possible shepherds such as these, half evil, half holy." In a dramatic audience with the czar he was able to cast suspicion on the work of Gossner and the Bible Society, portraying it as a conspiracy against the welfare of the Orthodox empire. Under the cloak of a religious movement a revolution was supposedly in the making. From Vienna, Metternich, who disagreed with Alexander's tolerant religious politics, contributed his share to the suspicions, and Alexander gave in. Gossner and Lindl were forced to leave the country. Back in Germany they took up duties with the Evangelical Lutheran Church, where Gossner was to contribute to the work of home missions.

Golitsin was compelled to resign and the Russian Bible Society to suspend its activities. In 1826 Alexander's creation was abolished by his successor Czar Nicholas I. Only five years later, however, the Evangelical Bible Society was founded, though under compulsion to limit its activities to the German-speaking congregations. Alexander I died in 1825 while on a visit to the Crimea, where he paid his respects at the grave of Julie de Krüdener. Did he indeed return to that mystic faith that had touched him so deeply ? It is not surprising that legends have been woven around his person. The story is told that the coffin in which the body of the deceased czar was brought to St. Petersburg was not opened and displayed in the Kazan cathedral, as was the custom. But in 1844, Fedor Kuzmich, a venerable old man, died in Siberia. He had come there as a stranger, and during twenty years had instructed children, taken care of the sick, and prayed for them. He was honored as a saint. When in 1933 the Soviet Government had the coffins of the deceased czars opened, the one engraved with the name of Alexander I was purportedly found empty.

The rule of Alexander's successor, Nicholas I, began with the suppression of the December Uprising. This was a prelude to a period of reactionary nationalism. Separated from the Russian church, the Protestants in their city congregations and colonies lived as in a confessional ghetto. Their spiritual influence in Russia was completely dammed up. Nevertheless, the history of the contact of Orthodox Russians with the Protestant revival in St. Petersburg had not come to an end. In the second half of the 19th century there was to be a continuation, or a new start, in one way or another building on what had taken place under Alexander. Who can judge what continued to live in the hidden recesses of the heart, to reappear anew at a given moment ?

IV. Stundism

Czar Alexander II (1855 - 1881) began his reign with the resolve to introduce the much-needed reforms for which a large segment of the population had longed for many years. One of his most important decrees was the abolition of serfdom in 1861. Millions of peasants were freed, yet many found it discouraging that they still had to pay for the land they received in compensation for their long servitude, and that therefore it would be many years before they were truly free of the village peasant community. In reality their land was now collectively owned, and they remained bowed under heavy burdens. The emancipation was not what they had dreamed it would be. Yet it is well to keep the fact of the peasants' emancipation in mind when we direct our attention to the religious movement which appeared among the peasants in southern Russia and the Ukraine at that time. We call this movement Stundism.

We have seen how *Bibelstunden* had become popular in the German colonies, particularly in Rohrbach under the influence of the Reformed minister Johann Bonekemper. His son Karl, who in 1867 became minister in the former pastorate of his father, continued these fellowship groups. Seasonal laborers from Russian and Ukrainian villages became involved in them, although that was really forbidden. They themselves began to hold meetings in their own homes, inspired by what they had seen and experienced with the Germans. The Rev. Mr. Bonekemper, however, constantly impressed upon them the need to remain faithful to the Orthodox Church. At first this was obvious to the peasants. They belonged to the church, and certainly had no intention of leaving it. Like the colonists, they wanted to hold their "meetings" within the framework of their own church. They continued faithfully to attend worship services on Sunday and holy days and partook of Holy Communion. Already in 1865 a priest had heard of their meetings, but did not judge them dangerous or sectarian. Another priest reported on a visit to those who took part in such conventicles as follows: [34]

> I myself was moved to tears, and several wept with me and assured me that they had never forsaken their faith. Further, they said that they had no set doctrine at all, and hence were unable to state from where and from whom they had received this so-called new doctrine, and that when they met together in their homes they did nothing except read from the holy Scriptures and sing spiritual songs, and therefore did not feel guilty.

The Stundists still belonged to the church and wished to live as Christians after the example of the German colonists. But the church's pastoral approach soon led to fierce contention. The village priests were not prepared to supply these church members in their spiritual need with wisdom and pastoral concern, nor to give the movement proper direction. They lacked the education for that, and because of their position in a ruling state church, the inner disposition as well. Generally they had received only a meager schooling in Christian doctrine and the performance of official duties, and lived as farmers among farmers. They did not enjoy very much respect among the people. A well-known Russian proverb went like this: "Intelligent as a parish priest — he sold his books and bought a deck of cards."[35] The priests soon tried to get the authorities to combat the new movement. Among the higher government agencies during the reign of Alexander II, there was a more liberal attitude as well as an awareness of the deficiencies of the clergy. One governor advised that well-educated priests be introduced because wrong convictions can be contested only by right convictions. "Alas, there are no such priests in the bishopric of Kherson." It became apparent that the farmers did not find in their own clergy those qualities which, on the basis of Holy Writ, they wanted to see. In a letter dated 1875 a judge wrote that one could not overcome this evil through administrative means.[36]

> It is in the deepest sense a natural reaction to the deep religious and moral ignorance of our people, to the failure of the leaders of their spiritual life and the pastoral instruction of the people in the truths of the Christian faith ... Very many of our priests set a bad example ... the people belong to the Orthodox Church only externally. Because the priesthood neglects its duty, it opens the way to all sorts of harmful ideas. The responsibility for the existence of so many sects rests with the priests, who neglect the preaching of the Christian faith and for whom religion is merely observing the ritual of the Orthodox Church.

There were those in the church who began to see this and who tried to introduce more spiritual weapons into the struggle. Lay fraternities arose in the 80s to try to teach the farmers reading and writing, to hold Bible lectures on Sunday, and to stress the importance of preaching. In the meantime, however, the reign of Alexander III had begun. Autocracy, Orthodoxy, and nationalism coincided in his

51

government to leave no room for people who wanted to read the Bible independently. Efforts were no longer directed to win them back to the church but to suppress them. Next to the emancipation of the serfs and the deficiencies of the village clergy, a third circumstance played a role in the rise of Russian Stundism, namely, the appearance of a translation of the Bible in the language of the Russian people. Despite the fact that the Russian Bible Society was made to stop its activities under Nicholas I, various theologians went ahead anyway with the work of translating the Bible, among them Archimandrite Makari and the Leningrad professor Pavski.[37] Finally the synod of the Russian church decided to take this work into its own hands. On Alexander II's coronation day the synod decided to have the translation done under its auspices. The intention was not to use this new translation in the worship services, where the Church Slavonic text would be maintained. They only wanted a Bible for family use, one which everyone could understand. Metropolitan Philaret of Moscow, who firmly believed in the renewing power of the Word of God and who had already played an important role in the first years of the Bible Society, became the leader. The translation took place in co-operation with the four religious academies in St. Petersburg, Moscow, Kiev, and Kazan. In 1860 the New Testament first made its appearance, then portions of the Old Testament were published, and in 1873 the entire work was finished. There are more connections with the work of the Bible Society begun under Alexander I. Bible distribution had continued among the non-Orthodox inhabitants of the empire. For sixty years, from the reign of Alexander I, the Scotch Bible colporteur Melville had given himself to this work. Crossing and recrossing the country, he found opportunity even under Nicholas I to distribute Bible portions to many Orthodox, his modest and careful behavior helping him to steer clear of the police. He never had, however, any direct ties with beginning Stundism. The cradle of that religious movement is to be found in Osnova, near the Reformed colony of Rohrbach, in the neighborhood of Odessa. In the homes of farmer Michail Ratushni and his friend Ivan Onishchenko, the inhabitants of the small village with its eighty small farms came together to read the Gospel and to sing spiritual songs.

It is difficult to say precisely when it began. In 1866 the first news items in the St. Petersburg newspapers appeared. Michael Klimenko, who carefully investigated the sources, places the beginning in 1861. From Osnova the movement spread to other villages. The Stundists were conspicuous by their serious lifestyle, their emphasis on the need for self-development, and their zeal to witness to the Gospel. The writer N. S. Leskov has written much about them. In his novel *The Unbaptized Pope* he speaks of a group in southern Russia responsible for giving completely new stimulus to the religious life there. He calls them "a sort of hermits living in the world." According to him they were somewhat puritan by nature, but each one was able to read and write. They used this knowledge to read the Word of God. Human tradition, to which the clergy was so tied, they considered spoiled and degenerate. They lived purely and set an excellent example in domesticity and industry. "Rumor has it that their ideas were inspired by the German colonists. From this the so-called Stunda originated."

Leskov has a more positive opinion of the Stundists than the priests, who had the impression that these believers rejected church ceremonies, no longer honored their icons, and discontinued prayers to the saints. They soon began to accuse the Stundists before the authorities, especially when the movement seemed to be spreading rapidly, through the influence of seasonal workers, to Kirovograd in the neighborhood of Old Danzig and to

Kiev. From a police report in 1868 we get an idea of how the police regarded this group.[38]

> They say the saints and the Mother of God are ordinary human beings like the others, and that they cannot be called upon as mediators before God. Each person must pray for himself and must not pin his hopes on the prayers of the saints. God must be worshipped in spirit and in truth: the external signs of worship are without significance. Thus the veneration of cross and icons is ineffective. One may not worship relics and it is a sin to indulge in excessive drinking.

The conventicles had developed into a fundamentalist reform movement. Official "warnings" to the apostates began around 1872 in an attempt to bring them back to the true faith. These "warnings" were far from gentle. Police inspector Popov, known as the "patriarch of the Stundists," stupid, malicious, and coarse, persecuted the Bible-believing wherever he could find them. In a St. Petersburg periodical of that day he is described as follows :

> Typical of the old breed of policemen from the days of serfdom, Popov struck terror in the hearts of the people. With four other policemen under his command, he entered homes and, finding no icons, began to beat the man and his wife and children in order to bring them back to Orthodoxy.

It was just this kind of action, however, that drove the Stundists in the direction of forming their own fellowships and separating from the church. Increasingly they articulated their faith in contrast to the faith of the priests, who in this way lost their authority completely. They began to see themselves as the true Christians who alone based their faith on the Gospel, and came to pay more and more attention to their own forms of congregational life. The icons played a remarkable role. In every Orthodox home the family icon stood in the corner, the center of spiritual life in the household. The Stundists were reproached for not revering the icons; to put them away meant to break with the church. In order to bring everything out in the open, the Stundists of Chaplinka, in November, 1872, deposited their icons at the belltower of the church, thereby formally acknowledging a break with the State Church.

While the Rev. Mr. Bonekemper had indeed overseen the theological education of some Russian brethren, the German colonists could ill afford to help the Stundists, or to incorporate them into the fellowship of their church. In a sense, they lived under a spiritual quarantine and would seriously jeopardize their position were they to join in evangelizing the Orthodox Russians. But the Stundists, estranged from their church and searching for an organization to unite their fellowships so that they could better withstand external pressures, quite naturally came under the influence of the Baptists.

As we have seen, some Baptists or Mennonites had adopted the custom of administering baptism by immersion. The German Baptist leader Oncken had visited southern Russia in 1867, and the Baptist movement was spreading in the colonies. Recognition by the government was received in 1879, making it possible for them to live their own religious life according to their convictions. In Karlovka, not far from one of the Baptist congregations, lived a Joachim Cymbal. Together with other villagers he was baptized in 1869. The story is told that he secretly joined himself to a group of German candidates for baptism so that he might receive baptism undetected. If the story is true, we may assume that the German leader who administered the baptism acted as if he noticed nothing. Cymbal became the one who in turn baptized other Stundists — here, presumably, lies the beginning of the

Baptist movement. Other influences also worked in that direction. The evangelist Jagub or Jakov Delyakovich Deljakov, a Syrian in the service of the American Presbyterian mission, had devoted himself, like Melville, to the work of Bible distribution throughout Russia.[39] In the Caucasian city of Tiflis the merchant Nikita I. Voronin (1840 - 1905) was deeply influenced by him. This Voronin belonged to the Molokani, who rejected baptism. In 1867, however, he had himself been baptized in the river in the neighborhood of Tiflis by the Lithuanian evangelist Martin Kalweit, after which he founded a Baptist congregation in Tiflis. This incident is considered the birth of their movement by present-day Baptists in Russia. The Baptist centennial was therefore celebrated in 1967. The movement spread especially among the Molokani, from which came such well-known leaders and evangelists as Vasili Gurevich Pavlov (1854 - 1924), later one of the most important leaders of the Baptist movement in Russia, and Prochanov, whom we shall meet later in St. Petersburg. The center of the Russian Baptist movement came to lie in the Caucasus. As early as 1884 the first independent conference of Russian baptized brethren, the first union of congregations, was formed, naturally without permission from the authorities.

The attraction of the Baptist movement for the Stundists and other evangelical Christians in Russia is understandable. The avenue leading to affiliation with the Reformed or Lutheran Church was, in a way, blocked for them. These churches were clearly regarded in Russia as churches for foreigners. As such they enjoyed freedom of worship as they pleased and to found congregations. They were not, however, absolutely free in the extent of their activity, and they were very reluctant to work among the Orthodox Russians or Ukrainians for fear of losing what freedom they had. The influence upon their environment that emanated from them was more or less accidental, certainly, for the most part, not consciously sought. Therefore they could not furnish a distinct contribution to the process of founding churches among the scattered groups of Stundists. That role fell to the Baptists, who from the middle of the preceding century had become active in a number of European countries. From the first Baptist congregation in Hamburg originating through the work of Johann Gerhard Oncken (1800 - 1882), there are clear lines of communication with the German colonies in Russia, Poland, and the Baltic countries. The Baptists were conspicuous for their cheerful missionary zeal and their fervent sense of calling, which refused to be quenched even though exposed to many persecutions in various parts of Europe. They felt themselves less restrained by diverse historically-created situations, and hence sought out the Stundists and devoted themselves to them without any internal inhibitions. But external causes alone did not determine development in the direction of the Baptists. Their attraction to the Baptist movement can be seen as an almost unavoidable reaction to the formalistic character of a state church in which membership was a certain and inescapable necessity for every Russian. In the *Stunden* the emphasis was on personal involvement with Christ, and a critical attitude toward the official church developed, a church which indeed administered baptism and observed the holy liturgy, but where less emphasis was placed on a personal faith. For the Stundists this personal faith became precisely the only basis for membership in the Christian church. Not the church, but each individual is the bearer of faith. The church is not, or *ought* not to be, an official institution, a part of the state apparatus. The church is the fellowship, the congregation of born-again Christians. This congregation is built upon the baptism of believers. Baptism takes place only if there is a personal experiencing and accepting of the salvation given in Christ, and is done through immersion. There

57

was no problem here for the Stundists, since in the Orthodox Church they had become acquainted with this mode of baptism; infant baptism in the Orthodox churches took place also by immersion, not through sprinkling. The baptism of believers and, bound up with it, closed Communion, to which only the baptized might come, made the difference between nominal Christians and the official church abundantly clear for the Stundists. Was it not the Orthodox Church that had treated them so shamefully and, by their very persecuting of these earnest Christians, alienated them from itself ? For with these persecutions the church was instrumental in driving the Stundists to organize their own congregations. A liberal newspaper in the 1870's wrote : [40]

> People who read the Gospel, who exert themselves to live according to the Word, as Christians, people who seek moral truth, but who do not feel at home in the formalism of religious ceremonies, honest, industrious, sober folk who perform all their duties to the state and society—these are the people we find in the defendant's bench.

It is perfectly understandable that these people should seek new forms of congregational life, and that they thought to find these among the Baptists.

The Reformed observer H. Dalton stated, moreover, that the more solid organization of the Baptists attracted the unorganized masses of ecclesiastically uprooted Stundists. They did not initially allow themselves to be baptized in large numbers, but slowly the Baptist movement spread over southern Russia. The intention was to organize congregations as they were founded in the New Testament. At the head was the presbyter and next to him at his side the deacon. These were not considered clergy, nor were they paid. Chosen from among the brotherhood by the fellowship, the presbyter baptized, led in public worship, and gave leadership to the life of the congregation.

Since the law forbade Russians to organize independent congregations, great problems arose in regard to the recording of births, marriages, and deaths. As there was no registry office, everyone had to turn to the priest. But the Stundists found this way closed to them. Already in 1873, when houses were searched, books were found in which secret records of birth and deaths were kept. Officially, however, one lived in concubinage and children were illegitimate if the marriage ceremony had not been performed by the priest.

Characteristic of Stundism already in that first period was a strong evangelism activity. No opportunity was neglected to bear witness to the faith in Christ, during work, for example, or when meeting others at inns, and also on the way to distant Siberia. The Russian Baptist movement from the beginning strived to unite the congregations in a union of churches. During times of serious persecution this unity helped them to continue visiting and supporting one another and thus they were better able to endure. For after Alexander III's accession to the throne in 1881, the measures taken by the authorities against the Stundists grew steadily more extreme. While in the beginning of the 80's they could still count somewhat on a certain sympathy in high government circles and were often acquitted in lawsuits, during the reign of Alexander III they lived in constant terror. Painful suffering began. The Stundists tried to get the law of 1879 officially recognizing the Baptists declared applicable also to themselves. But they were regarded as Stundo-Baptists and the law of 1893 against the Stundists was enforced in all its rigor. Gutsche in his book on Stundism[41] cites a part of this law.

> The children of the Stundists must be taken away
> from their parents and entrusted to relatives who

are members of the Orthodox Church; if there
are no relatives, then they must be entrusted to
the parish clergy.

Henceforth the Stundists are forbidden to hold
church services or to organize schools.

Stundist passports and birth certificates must
mention the fact that they belong to this sect.
A proprietor who hires a Stundist will be
punished with a high fine. The names of the
members of this sect must be referred to the
ministry of travel, where they shall have the list
posted in railway stations so that they can no
longer travel. A Stundist may not take an
Orthodox believer into his employ. Infringement
of the law will be punished with exile to the
Caucasus for five years. Stundists are not permitted to buy or rent real estate. A Stundist
found in the company of others during Bible
reading and prayer must be arrested and, in
accordance with administrative form, exiled
immediately to Siberia. A preacher must be condemned to hard labor in the Siberian mines.
Stundists may not be buried in the sacred soil
of the cemetery; no funeral service may be conducted for them.

And this decree did not remain a dead letter. Children
were taken away, men and women were locked up in
prisons or exiled to Siberia. The law was applied to the
full. Only underground were certain contacts possible;
despite great difficulties, fraternal conferences continued
annually. But even in exile they maintained their activity.
When he had served his sentence in 1895, Pavlov left a
group of 150 baptized members behind him in Orenburg
in Siberia. Up until 1905 it was dangerous to be a Stundist, but in that year the czar relented and a period of
relative freedom began. For those who had suffered so

much during the regimes of the czars, the revolution of 1917 came as a real liberation. It was not for their political views that the Stundists were persecuted, though they were sometimes accused of nihilism by the authorities in order to justify the persecutions. The Stundists did not pursue political interests and social reforms. Above all else they wanted to remain true to their faith and preach the Gospel as they had come to know it. They wanted also to organize their churches according to the insights they had found in the Bible. While freedom to do that was not granted under the czars, there was a short period immediately after the Revolution (up to 1929) in which they could come into their own. Then again the night of persecutions descended. The title given a writing in 1967 in commemoration of the centennial of the Baptist movement in Russia is, alas, perfectly in place: "One Hundred Years of Struggle and Suffering."

V. The Raskol in High Society

In his book *Resurrection* Tolstoy relates how the main character visited a revival meeting in St. Petersburg at the home of a countess where a certain Kiesewetter was to speak. After an excellent dinner the public gathered in the large drawing room.

> Near the drive, splendid carriages stood, and ladies in silk, velvet and lace with wigs and false bosoms entered the salon. Among the ladies a few gentlemen also were seated and there were military men and citizens and five very ordinary fellows, two house servants, a shopkeeper, a coachman, and a clerk. Kiesewetter, a vigorous elderly man, spoke only in English, and a pale girl with a fancy pair of glasses translated quickly and fluently. He spoke about the sins of man as being so great and the punishments for them so heavy that it was impossible to comprehend them. "If only we give some thought to ourselves, beloved brethren and sisters, we shall clearly understand that there is no forgiveness for us, and no rescue, but that we are all doomed." He stopped and one could hear sobbing. The countess sat by a small mosaic table with her head resting on both arms and her

well-rounded shoulders convulsing. The coach-
man looked at the preacher with amazement and
fright, as if he had made for him with the
carriage pole and the man couldn't get out of the
way. The majority of the guests were in the
same condition as Countess Tsaiky.

Suddenly the lecturer looked up. As he did so, a
smile that looked real came over his face, the
kind that theatrical players summon to express
joy. And then he continued with a tender,
engaging voice: "And yet there is deliverance.
It is easy and comforting and rests on the blood
of the only begotten Son of God who out of love
offered Himself and poured out His blood for
us . . ."

It is quite clear from this description that Tolstoy was not
much impressed by the English preacher he pictures here.
He gives a somewhat satirical description of the meeting
held in the home of the countess and considers the preaching one-sided and sectarian. His own spiritualist-moralist
conception of faith left little room for appreciation of the
way the Gospel was preached here.

We can assume that in depicting this preacher Tolstoy
had in mind the English revival preacher Granville
Augustus William Waldegrave, the third Baron Radstock
(1833 - 1916). Lord Radstock had come to St. Petersburg
at the invitation of a lady who had met him in Paris, so
that he might bring the Gospel there too. After his conversion he had devoted himself completely to the work of
evangelism among those of his own class. At first connect-
ed with the Plymouth Brethren, he now worked
independently and was not supported by any group.

In 1874 he came to St. Petersburg and held meetings
in the little English Church and in the salons of the St.
Petersburg aristocracy. The fact that he spoke in English

and French presented no difficulty in those circles. His personality, according to some critical observers, was more captivating than his sermons. Not only Tolstoy, but also N. S. Leskov has written about him. Leskov, who carefully followed the religious life of his day, wrote fully about Radstock, among others, in his *Velikosvetski Raskol*—the separation (*raskol*) in high society. The book was extremely critical and ridiculed Radstock's dry sermons and his limited knowledge of theology, which comprised hardly more than a primitive conception of justification by faith. For Radstock, however, he had more appreciation.[42] He wrote:

> His ideas don't amount to much but his feelings are beautiful, and his success fully justifies the words of Taine that people allow themselves to be swept away not by ideas but by their feelings. Merely to look at him is an inspiration. You cannot for a moment doubt that this man lives through the Spirit and cares about people with all his heart, and when he bids farewell to his guide and disappears behind the heavily-draped door of his hotel, you feel that you have just said goodbye to the best and most upright man among all those with whom you ever had to do.

An accurate picture of Radstock conducting a meeting can be found in a little book by the princess Sophie Lieven entitled *A Seed That Bore Rich Fruit*.[43] In a charming manner this Russian princess near the end of her life describes the experiences of her youth. Her Orthodox mother Nathalia and her aunt Princess Gagarin soon joined the group which attended Lord Radstock's meetings. Both were to continue to play an important role, especially in the later years of persecution. Her father, chief master of ceremonies at the court of Czar Alexander II, was Lutheran, from a Baltic family that had had many connections with Pietism. The children by a mixed marriage were, of course, Orthodox. But in these circles intensive contact between Orthodox and Lutheran took place. Moreover, Russian noblemen frequently stayed in Western Europe, and some of them had come into contact there with the revival movements within Protestantism. One member of Radstock's circle, for example, was a lady who had come to the faith through the preaching of the evangelist Moody. Princess Lieven knew all those who had come under the influence of Lord Radstock's preaching. Among them, Colonel Pashkov undoubtedly held first place. He was to become the soul of a new religious movement. Vasili Aleksandrovich Pashkov (1831-1902), a former officer in the imperial guard, was a very wealthy man with vast estates and owned copper mines in the Urals.

> One day, according to Princess Lieven, Lady Pashkov invited Lord Radstock to dinner. The colonel, who was not much attracted by the preaching of the English lord, nonetheless as host had to receive him. At the table God's Word was discussed, and the guest told about his life's experiences and tried to show those present the joy of being saved. After dinner the company retired to the elegant salon, where the conversation was continued. Colonel Pashkov listened carefully but the subject meant little to him. When Lord Radstock suddenly proposed that they kneel for a prayer, it displeased the colonel greatly. He had never seen such a thing before. As an Orthodox believer he was accustomed to kneel in church or in his room before an icon and repeat certain prescribed prayers. But simply to kneel with guests in the salon and to address God in his own words seemed highly improper. Out of courtesy he doubtlessly kneeled, but only very reluctantly.

And yet, when he heard that man pray so fervently for those present, his heart was deeply touched and light began to flood his soul. Suddenly it became clear to him that this concerned him personally. He was the lost sinner the Gospels were talking about; as the lost son he must repent. In that moment he saw the complete hopelessness of his condition, but also that there was forgiveness with God only through the suffering and death of Jesus Christ.

From that moment one can speak of a genuine revival movement. For Pashkov took the spiritual leadership of the group upon himself, together with Count A. P. Bobrinski and Count Modest Korff, who filled a high position at the court and was already deeply involved with the distribution of the Bible.

Lord Radstock remained a half year in St. Petersburg and then left to return a year later for a longer period. Pashkov's home on the Neva quay became a real center of evangelism. Evening meetings were organized in which people of the highest status came together for Bible discussions. With servants also invited, it soon became a very mixed company that gathered together. Pashkov brought the movement to the people. Sunday schools were organized, sometimes in private homes, where ten children might meet. The servant staff of the Lieven family alone numbered, with their families, more than fifty persons. Pashkov was an inspiring and socially concerned person. Leskov says of him: "He is an upright and fervent man, prepared to give himself completely to what he considers the truth." And he did just that. An area of social concern —or perhaps we can better call it a charitable concern— developed. Eating houses for the poor and for the students were opened. Sewing classes during which the Bible was read were organized for girls and women. A girls' society was formed. Ladies' committees assumed responsibility for visiting prisoners and the sick. And of course there were the inevitable bazaars.

The Pashkovites, as they were sometimes called, sprang up also outside of St. Petersburg. Pashkov evangelized not only in hospitals and prisons but also on his estates. His great generosity often brought confusion to his land agents. There was much singing at the meetings. Revival songs were translated from English and German, and the father-in-law of Count Korff, Shulepnikov, composed new hymns and psalm melodies. Financial means were not lacking, but more important was the great enthusiasm with which Bibles, tracts, and the evangelism journal *The Russian Laborer* were distributed. They knew how to make the most of opportunities. When one day a squadron of Pashkov's former regiment passed by his house, he asked the commanding officer whether he might distribute New Testaments to the soldiers. The officer gave his permission — he could hardly do otherwise for his former superior—and each soldier received a little Bible. It must have been a striking incident, discussed at large.

Less striking was the work performed by F. W. Baedeker. Closely allied to the Pashkovites, he went on to work entirely by himself. He was a friend of Lord Radstock, of German descent but of English upbringing. He spent many years in Russia visiting prisoners. A remarkable man, trusted by the authorities, he spoke little about his own experiences but became a blessing to many. He distributed little Bibles and tracts and spoke to the prisoners of the love of God. With the text "God is love"—Bog yest lyubov—which is now written above the pulpit in many Evangelical Christian and Baptist churches, he began his discourses, which were translated by his companion L. V. Kargel, later one of the leading brethren in St. Petersburg. We probably meet Baedeker in Tolstoy's *Resurrection* when we are told that in a Siberian prison the main character meets an Englishman who visits prisoners, preaches, and hands out Bibles. He paraphrases his discourse: "Tell them that Christ has pity on them and loves them and has died for them. If they believe that, they shall be saved."

There were more of these silent witnesses. Baron P. N. Nikolai, who began a Christian student movement in St. Petersburg and later invited John Mott and Sherwood Eddy to visit him, was among the faithful members of the Evangelical Christians, as they began to call themselves. At first calling themselves Christians-according-to-the-Gospel, they later chose the name Evangelical Christians, based on Acts 11: 26 and Philippians 1: 27. In those first years there was no question of an organized congregational alliance. They did celebrate communion at the meetings and there were, indeed, some who after their conversion were baptized anew — Pashkov for example, who was baptized by George Miller from Bristol when he visited Russia in 1882. Gradually, however, under the leadership of Pashkov there arose a council of brethren that gave guidance to congregational life. But many still maintained a formal bond with the State Church.

Pashkov was very anxious to make contacts with other evangelical groups in Russia and was particularly interested in the Stundists. Those of the nobility in St. Petersburg who had been touched by the revival tried as much as possible to help the Stundists, many of whom had been imprisoned. The wife of the chief of police, a member of the group, was in a position to help many Stundists. After Pashkov had sent out many letters of invitation, some seventy brethren from all over Russia came together on April 1, 1884, to talk with one another about co-operation and unity. Among them were also Molokani and Baptists. But after two days the meeting was disrupted by the police, who now also took measures against the St. Petersburg aristocrats. Mainly because of their contacts with the Stundists, they had come under suspicion of engaging in activities which were detrimental to state and church. Count Korff and Colonel Pashkov were ordered to appear before the Minister of Justice, where they were instructed to promise not to preach any more, not to hold meetings, not to pray in their own words, and to break all contacts with the Stundists and other religious fellowships. When they refused, they were banished from the country. They died in exile. In 1902 Pashkov was buried in Rome. At his grave the minister read the text: "Blessed are they which are persecuted for righteousness' sake, for theirs is the kingdom of heaven" (Matt. 5: 10). Count Bobrinski meanwhile retired to his estates.

But even though the evangelical movement in St. Petersburg came under strict supervision by the Orthodox state, the work secretly continued. The meetings went on in the house of Princess Lieven, who in the meantime had become a widow, but also in other sections of the city in homes of the less distinguished. Up to 1905 they bore more or less an underground character.

Princess Lieven did not allow herself to be intimidated by a messenger from the government but remained a tower of strength for the congregations. She was also the first to inform the congregation of the Toleration Act of 1905 that finally brought freedom and recognition to the oppressed groups. An eyewitness tells it like this: [44]

> Princess Lieven was informed of the decision of the czar. However, she said nothing to the participants at a conference of brethren held in those days, but invited them to gather on Easter morning at 6 o'clock in the grand salon of her palace. They were all present. Then the princess entered the room, dressed in white and wearing the crown on her head, the imperial edict in her trembling hands. She read it to all. An indescribable moment. Before the clocks began to toll,

before everyone else knew the good news that would be made known, we were on our knees thanking God for the liberation of our brothers and sisters who sighed in exile.

But for the present, things had not yet gone that far. Difficult times were still to come.

The leadership gradually passed over into the hands of the "simple, less educated folk," as Princess Lieven wrote. The well-to-do always spent the summer on their estates; thus their less privileged brothers, present summer and winter, were in a better position to determine the shape of congregational life, and exercise a greater influence in the church council. As the wavering fell away, it became clear that for the furtherance of congregational life, particularly in a time of stress and persecution, a stiffer organization was necessary.

Already at that time Ivan Stepanovich Prochanov (1869 - 1935) began to play an important role, giving guidance to the life of evangelical Christians. He came from a Molokani family that had joined the Baptist movement. In 1893 he illegally went to Western Europe, where he studied theology and tried to arouse sympathy for his persecuted fellow believers. Upon his return in 1898 he found a position with an American technical firm and continued to devote himself completely to the cause of the Gospel. Before Czar Nicholas II announced the Toleration Act, he had taken the opportunity to publish a collection of hymns including several of his own. Thereby he laid the foundation for a treasury of hymns for evangelical Christians. He published periodicals but focused his attention especially on the work of evangelism, the upbuilding and organization of congregational life, and the gathering together of scattered groups into the union of Evangelical Christians.

It was no simple task to try to bring together the two currents, the one from the south and the other from the

St. Petersburg area. Leskov, who observed both movements, had more sympathy for the Stundists than for the Pashkovites. He wrote to a friend in 1874 :

> I want to devote a study to them, entitled *Practical Christians In Southern Russia*. I have been there and have observed this Stundism, and I am convinced that it is genuine piety originating not so much from strange influences as from a neglect of practical activity in the Orthodox communion.

He spoke continually of the contrast between the peasant Stundists and the "sentimental piety" of the aristocratic followers of Lord Radstock, which he considered only a hazy mysticism that would not long endure after the exile of Pashkov. Such an evaluation, however, undoubtedly does an injustice to a man like Pashkov and does not correctly plumb the real depth of the Gospel movement in St. Petersburg. Pashkov carried on an extensive correspondence with him about this. Leskov did not understand this movement, w h i c h R. Stupperich characterizes as "new Methodism."[45] The Pashkovite movement had more significance than Leskov and other critical contemporaries supposed.

Begun in the salons, it grew into a popular movement, one more protest against certain aspects and shortcomings of the State Church. For even though the Russian church in different ways experienced a lively theological development in the 19th century, yet as a result of its ties with the government and its functioning as the official ideology of the czarist autocratic rule, it was greatly checked in its development. In common, everyday church life there was too much concern about form and religious ceremony. As N. Arseniev writes : [46]

> Two dangers threatened the religious life of the Russian church: on the one hand, the great importance sometimes attached to the external

71

forms of public worship, an aesthetic and formalistic tendency; on the other hand, the excessive influence of the state on the life of the church, especially since the reform movement of Peter the Great.

With the Evangelical Christians we see a process of interiorization, and certainly in the beginning a one-sided emphasis on socially-oriented work. Determined by the outlook of that time, the work of domestic and city missions, developed under the impetus of Protestant non-Russians, had taken on considerable proportions. Dalton writes in his *Life's Reminiscences*: [47]

> According to the laws of the land, our city mission might labor only among our own fellow believers. To respond to the oft-heard call "Come over and help us" was considered (by the watchmen of the State Church) an overstepping of the boundaries of a foreign confession. If only they had undertaken a similar work among themselves.

This work, then, the Pashkovites engaged in, and it lifted the movement above the vague mysticism of which Leskov had unjustly accused them. Above all, they were a Bible-oriented movement which sought to promote the independent use of the Scriptures. It was this that united them with the brethren in the south despite all the differences that existed. After the period of suppression it was evident that the Baptist current there had gained the upper hand and was the most determinative. In the north this was less pronounced. There were, indeed, groups that had accepted adult baptism by immersion and advocated the stricter congregational pattern of the Baptists. But Prochanov, though closely allied to the Baptist movement, nonetheless advocated a more gradual development and a less rigid pattern of congregational life. He had made it his goal to bring the two currents together in one common bond but had dedicated himself, first of all, to unifying the congregations of the Evangelical Christians. Anyway, the differences in origin of the two currents were too great, particularly in the beginning, to make direct and complete unity possible. Only after a second period of suppression and persecution under the Soviets would the two evangelical movements in the south and north find each other in the formation of the Union of Evangelical Christians and Baptists in 1944.

VI. The Molokani

Many of those who study the life within the Christian church in Russia tend to view the Evangelical Christians and Baptists as groups of western origin. W. Kolarz, who has written one of the best-documented books on the religious life in the Soviet Union from 1917 to 1957, writes about them in a chapter entitled "Western Protestantism."[48] He immediately emphasizes, however, that there is a certain synthesis of Western Protestantism with Russian and Ukrainian piety.

In his book *La Vie Religieuse en U.R.S.S.,*[49] Constantin de Grunwald, well-known French writer of Russian descent, adopts a most remarkable point of view. He considers the hostile attitude of the Soviet authorities toward the Evangelical Christians and Baptists sufficiently justified by the American connections of the Baptist Church, and is convinced that the patriarchate of the Russian Orthodox Church could hardly be expected to sympathize with these anti-sacramentalists who rob them of so many believers. According to him, the Baptists' greatest handicap is their foreign origin. Their fellowship came into existence through foreign influence and continues to exist under foreign influence. Does it contain enough elements, he asks himself, to reach the masses of a people whose religious feeling is so closely bound to national consciousness and ancestral traditions? De Grunwald, however, really does what so many Russian emigrants have done in the last fifty years. Theologians and religious philosophers have projected a certain image of Russia and of Russian piety, from which one gets the impression of a sort of natural alliance between Russia and Orthodoxy. The Russian soul for them is naturally Orthodox. They have contributed, says Ernst Benz,[50] to the rise "of the myth of an unbroken Christianity of the Russian man." That perception, however, neglects two factors, namely, the influence of atheistic propaganda, of the dialectic-materialistic catechism that for fifty years has made its impact and in which everyone is educated "from cradle to grave"; and the influence of modern secularized technical-scientific culture, which in every country and certainly also in Russia has displaced old culture patterns. The fact is that Russia for many centuries has experienced a certain isolation and was able with some success to ward off influences from the outside. Moreover, there is a traditional historical alliance between the Orthodox Church and the Russian people that actually remained inviolate from the establishment of the Russian state up to the Revolution. In the 19th century especially that unbroken unity of people and church expressed itself in a particularly evil manner, as we have already seen, in the suppression and isolation of nonconforming believers. But that a movement's foreign origin would handicap it in its efforts to reach the Russian people is sufficiently belied by the influence which Marxism has been able to get. De Grunwald's outlook is highly debatable. Moreover, he borrows an argument that atheistic propaganda has frequently used, that is, the so-called American connections of the Baptists. His reference is to a nonentity, for American influences on the growth of the Evangelical Christians and Baptists in Russia have been totally lacking. Naturally these groups wanted, where possible, to maintain contacts with fellow believers in other parts of the world. Not so strange, really, for Christians. The discussion of the foreign origin of the Evangelical Christians and Baptists would seem comparable to a discussion of whether Protestantism in Holland is of French or German origin. Naturally there have been such influences, but the Reformation found a ready response in Holland and a soil in which it could grow. So it was also in Russia. Of course there have been influences emanating from Western European Protestantism. Russia is a European country, and despite its isolated position, could never completely shut itself off from fertilization by foreign currents and ideas. In the preceding chapters we have seen something of that and have established the fact that sparks indeed blew over. As it is written in the Gospel of John (3: 8): "The wind bloweth where it listeth, and thou hearest the sound thereof, but canst not tell whence it cometh, and whither it goeth: so is everyone that is born of the Spirit." This is verified in the history of the rise of the Protestant movement in Russia. There have been contacts with immigrant churches—could the attention attracted by the sober-living, pious Protestant peasants have been avoided? How could others not begin to ask themselves what inspired these folk as they gathered together about the Bible, without ceremony, but "with gladness and singleness of heart"? There were those like Radstock and Baedeker, Melville and Kalweit who traveled through Russia with the Bible. They did not want to found churches but in their own way to witness to Christ. People listened to them and even began to read the Bible for themselves. The rise of Protestant currents within Russia largely parallels the distribution of the Bible and its translation into the Russian spoken language. But that does not mean that the Evangelical Christians and Baptists are of a strange, foreign origin. That non-Orthodox means the same as non-Russian is a nationalistic misconception arising out of the old monopolistic attitude of a state-church Christianity and is, moreover, an historical inaccuracy. Before there was any question of Baptists and Evangelical Christians, there were groups of people in Russia who had left the State Church and as free churches or sects lived their own life. Among them were those who displayed a decidedly Protestant character. Russian soil has been unusually fertile for the development of sects," the term by which all these groups that stand outside any connection with the State Church are called in Russia. Among them are groups on which we also inaccurately pin that label, as well as groups, such as the Molokani, we probably would not call sects. Many Russian "sects" have a character of their own and are difficult to compare with sectarian or separatist groups in the West. Each church has its own divisions, its own alternative groups. And the Orthodox Church of Russia has had many of them. According to R. A. Klostermann,[51] the Orthodox Church more than any other has given birth to sects.

The most important separation is that of the conservative Old-Believers, who rejected the reforms that Patriarch Nikon introduced in 1654 in favor of keeping the old Orthodox ways. They exist up to the present day. Another important group is that of the Molokani, who exhibit a distinct Protestant character. The roots of this group reach far into the past. During the reign of Czar Peter, strong Protestant tendencies were noticeable in Russia. Bishop Feofan Prokopovich, who administered many of Czar Peter's reforms, taught that Holy Scripture is the only foundation of faith. The physician Dmitri Tveretinov[52] also labored during this time, proclaiming a "strange doctrine" by interpreting Bible passages along "Protestant" lines and presenting them as doctrine of faith. He rejected the ecclesiastical tradition, the veneration of Mary and the saints, religious relics and icons, and monastic vows. Because of these views, however, he

77

got himself into grave trouble in 1713, and only through the personal intervention of Czar Peter was he able to save his life.

But his writings continued to exert their influence. Werner Krause[53] considers the Molokani Tveretinov's spiritual descendants. The group originated later under the influence of the preaching of Simeon Uklein in Tambov in the middle of the 18th century. He also proclaimed that the Bible was the only source of doctrine and that it alone had authority in matters of faith. He opposed the State Church with its sacraments, rituals, veneration of saints and icons. According to him, the church fathers had mixed the pure Word of God with Greek philosophy and thereby had polluted the faith. He rejected war and the military draft and taught that all men are equal. On the lower Volga he founded a Christian commune. He and his followers were persecuted, of course, but in the beginning of the 19th century, under Alexander I, they received official recognition.[54] They took an active part in the Bible distribution that was carried on by the Russian Bible Society at that time. Calling themselves "spiritual Christians," they were generally called by others Molokani, a name derived from the Russian word *moloko* meaning "milk," which name probably originated from their custom of drinking only milk during feasts. They themselves say that this name was given them because their doctrine is the "spiritual milk" that Paul speaks of in I Cor. 3: 2. Referring to John 4: 24, "God is a Spirit and they that worship him must worship in spirit and in truth," they reject outward church forms; baptism for them is like prayer. Their liturgy is limited to the reading of the Bible, to its exposition, and to the singing of spiritual songs, primarily Psalms or portions of the Epistles sung to a monotonous, melancholy melody. Their congregations are built along Presbyterian lines and each member is competent to preach. The

78

Molokani are very conservative and puritanical and take no part in the general cultural life around them. Molokani congregations still exist in Russia, for example, in Baku and Tiflis. While at the beginning of this century their number was estimated at one million believers, membership has dropped drastically since then. To a large extent they have been absorbed by the Baptists and Evangelical Christians.

It is inaccurate to present matters as if these Protestant groups live on imported conceptions of faith that are strange to their own Russian piety. The Molokani are genuine Russian believers, without foreign, Western European, or — worse — American "stains." Originating within the climate of the Orthodox Church, they confronted that church with their beliefs and separated themselves from what they considered erroneous in that church according to the Bible as they understood it. In their spiritualistic conception of faith they can be considered a reaction to the formalism of the official church.

The Baptists and Evangelical Christians won their first followers among the Molokani, from whom some of their leading figures originated. N. I. Voronin, baptized in Tiflis in 1867 and regarded as the first Russian Baptist, belonged originally, like Masayev and Pavlov, to the Molokani. Pavlov, the first Baptist leader, writes in his reminiscences: [55]

> My parents were Molokani. This sect is almost Protestant, but like the Quakers they reject baptism and the Lord's Supper. I became convinced that I should be baptized. I joined the Baptist fellowship in Tiflis in 1870, at the age of sixteen. The group had just been formed and consisted only of a few people. My parents were opposed to what I did.

Evangelical Christians and Baptists in our day, such as

Y. Zhidkov and A. Karev, are proud of their Molokanish descent. By pointing to this descent they probably want to indirectly counteract the accusations that their movement is foreign-inspired, which accusations were used again and again in czarist times and by Soviet propaganda as a motive for suppressing them.

The origin of these Protestant currents in Russia, however, is never to be solely explained in terms of cultural and religious infiltration from Western Europe. While in one sense they were a protest movement against the form the church had received in their countries, in a more important sense they emerged as a current that sought to handle the Scriptures differently than was customary in actual practice in Russian church life. That they finally established themselves as independent groups beside the Orthodox Church is due in large measure to the way in which the church treated these believers.

The Evangelical Christians and Baptists in Russia are to be regarded as a lay movement. Their concept of the ministry is poorly developed, and lay activity is deliberately encouraged. This is quite contrary to the Orthodox Church, which has in practice a strong official and clerical character. All the emphasis there is placed on celebrating the liturgy, which for them is a constantly repeated theophany, a descent of God to His church. Since the 14th century what was essential in the liturgy has come to be hidden more and more behind the iconostasis, the icon screen that separates the altar from the congregation. Great difference exists too with regard to congregational singing, of which the Orthodox Church, which relies on choirs, knows little.

Already in the 14th century there is mention of a lay movement, the Strigolniki, possessing an anti-clerical character and exhibiting similarities with the Waldensians.[56] They focused their attention on abuses among the priests and were against the ordination of priests. Two leaders of this movement were drowned in the river Volkhov in 1375. Appearing chiefly in Novgorod and Pskov, the movement did not get a chance to develop. Much later, the idealistic theology of the Slavophiles in the 19th century, of which the lay theologian A. S. Chomyakov was the most important representative, rejected the official hierarchical conception of the church. For him the church is an organism growing together in a love and solidarity which all members share. He introduced the concept *sobornost*—fellowship in which everyone, bishops and lay members, has his place. Chomyakov has a particularly rich and evangelical-catholic conception of the church, but it has not been able really to permeate and renew the actual practice of Russian church life. We in the West must not too quickly associate the 19th-century practice of Russian church life with the thinking of Russian Orthodox theologians, which was often profound and inspiring. The church in pre-revolutionary Russia was part of an authoritarian government arrangement and its leadership an organ of the state. A deep life of faith and great spiritual strength inherent in the Russian church became evident in the times of persecution following the Revolution. But it has not been able to make room for such lay movements as Stundism and Pashkovism. The Orthodox Church in the 19th century had difficulty with the plurality of spiritual life it encountered and set itself in opposition to movements which might have been able to renew it.

The Evangelical Christians and Baptists distinguish themselves also by their strong emphasis on a consciously taken faith decision and a personal salvation experience. But here too there is no absolute contradiction with the teachings of Orthodoxy. Anyone who has attended an Orthodox church service and has witnessed the intense devotion of the believers can judge that for himself. We may regard the Baptists with their emphasis on adult baptism and the long period of preparation for that event as an alternative tendency within a church of pronounced people's-church character, as the church in Russia was in the pre-revolutionary period. As a matter of course, everyone was included in the church from birth. Furthermore, the church, despite the revival of church schools in the course of the 19th century, had only a poorly educated corps at its disposal. The parish priest had relatively little theological and pastoral knowledge and could scarcely meet and guide the religious emancipation movement. In the celebration of the liturgy the devout experiencing of the mystery of God's presence was central, not preaching or instruction in the faith. Catechetical instruction and pastoral care fell short, and those who sought a more direct association with the Bible as the Word of God became therein estranged from the church.

For the movements of the Evangelical Christians and Baptists are Bible movements. The rise of these currents parallels the appearance of the Bible in the language of the people. That is not to say that the Bible is a forgotten book in the Orthodox Church. The entire liturgy desires to do nothing else than to give form and substance to the evangelical message. There is no absolute antithesis between the Orthodox Church and the Evangelical Christians and Baptists, as we said before. But the old Church Slavonic Bible used in the church service is more suited to underline the mystery of the faith than to convey the Biblical message. The direct interpretation of Scripture receives little emphasis in the Orthodox Church. Among the Evangelical Christians and Baptists a deep longing was felt to make the Bible central in their lives and in the life of the church.

The Biblical message is many-voiced. It has been said that Peter is the teacher of the Roman Catholic Church, Paul the teacher of the Reformation, and John the teacher of Orthodoxy. Continuing in this vein, one might say that the Russian Evangelical Christians and Baptists within Johannine Christianity allowed the Pauline note to sound through: the justification of the sinner through faith in the saving act of God in Jesus Christ.

In dealing with these currents we are not concerned with some kind of anti-Orthodox movement but with a Bible-inspired movement that, alas, has come to stand outside the church. Not because they were touched by unfamiliar Western ideas but because the unfamiliar Word captivated them in a new way, they traveled their own difficult road.

Part II

VII. After the Revolution

The period of relative forbearance under the czarist regime from 1905 to 1914 gave the persecuted Stundists and Evangelical Christians the opportunity to make a new beginning with the building up of congregational life. In 1905 the Federation of Russian Baptists was founded, an event for which the first stone was laid already in 1884. D. I. Masayev from Rostock on the Don became both first chairman and editor of the periodical *The Baptist*. Prochanov, already in 1906, began to publish his paper *The Christian,* and in 1909 he founded the All-Russian Federation of Evangelical Christians. Thousands of brethren returned home from prisons and penal camps. The work could begin once more. Fifty evangelists were immediately sent out by the Baptists and a training center was begun. But the czarist administration continued to find it difficult to permit religious freedom in actual practice. Accordingly, all sorts of hindrances were laid in the way of these sectarians, as they were called. The outbreak of war put an end to this limited toleration. Preachers were again apprehended, Baptists were persecuted as "German believers" and were again forced to go underground.

For these groups, the persecuted stepchildren of Father Czar, the revolution of 1917 came as a liberation. The Communists knew them from the penal colonies where they had worked side by side with the believing Christians. Their anti-God stance and measures were directed especially against the Orthodox Church that had bound itself to the rule of the czar and had clearly adopted a highly disapproving attitude toward the revolutionaries. Lenin's decree of January 23, 1918, regarding the separation of church and state and of school and church was a frontal attack on the wealthy, privileged State Church. All financial aid to the church stopped; church buildings and other church properties were declared to belong to the state. Church buildings and objects for public worship might again be put at the disposal of the religious fellowship by the local or central government agency. But all church functionaries lost their state's income and the right to live in the parsonages that had become state property. The freedom of religious and anti-religious propaganda was firmly established in the constitution. But none of these restrictive measures had really anything to do with the Evangelical Christians and Baptists who owned neither church buildings nor parsonages and had never enjoyed a single privilege under czarist regime. In a retrospective on their hundred-year history illegally published in 1967 by a separate group of Evangelical Christians and Baptists, it was said that there had been only one period of freedom during the hundred-year road of suffering: [57]

> In the Soviet decree regarding "the separation of church and state and of school and church" of January 23, 1918, religious freedom was announced. Established in the constitution in Article 13 on freedom of conscience, this decree gave all citizens the freedom of religious and antireligious propaganda. Thus the next twenty years in the life of our fellowship were years of

favorable possibilities for the proclamation of the Gospel. The spreading of the message of salvation was highly successful in this time; it reached the far-distant cities of Siberia and central Asia, of the territory in the Far East, of the Ukraine and White Russia.

In most surveys of Russian church history the time after the Revolution is seen solely in the light of the fierce conflict between the new regime and the old State Church. In many ways, naturally, this conflict was the most characteristic feature of church history in Russia. But the history of the Evangelical Christians and Baptists is really the opposite of that of the State Church. If before 1917 they were oppressed and persecuted, now they profited in certain ways from the changed situation and could freely unfurl their banner in every direction. The anti-religious propaganda, aimed largely at the externals of the Orthodox Church, its connection with the czarist regime, its wealth, the attitude of the clergy, the external form of public worship and church life, nowhere implicated the Evangelical Christians and Baptists. They had belonged to the persecuted, they had the same objections to Orthodoxy, and the great majority of them came from the lower classes, from workmen and peasants. Lenin's new political economics from 1921 on was geared especially to winning the agrarian population for the regime, and its closely related liberalization ushered in a short period of prosperity in the life of the Russian "sectarians" who, particularly in the country, had a large following. In the Communist Party itself there was an important current that wanted to build up the Soviet state by incorporating in a positive way those formerly persecuted. "We must try to direct the immense economic and cultural possibilities of the sectarians within the channels of the Soviet program. Since the sectarians are many, this endeavor is very important." Thus ran a resolution by the

13th Congress of the Communist Party in 1923.[58] The expectations of the Evangelical Christians and Baptists were high. As late as the beginning of 1929, I. S. Prochanov wrote in the preface of his book *Erfolge des Evangeliums in Russland*: [59]

> The history of the Reformation is well known. Through her, God broke the powers of darkness and fanaticism in the old church, and brought freedom to believe and think to ultimate victory. Now it is Russia's turn. After the world-shocking events of the last war and of the Revolution, the evangelical movement is beginning to develop in the East in a very special way. Independently of the traditions of the old church, the Gospel is now preached soundly and purely in Russia.

Every now and then the Gospel picture of the grain of seed that is going to bear rich fruit comes to the fore. People saw the fields white unto harvest and went out into the limitless spaces of Russia. The work of evangelism was begun with diligence. Bibles were printed and distributed, and the work of translating into the many languages spoken within the Russian empire was begun. In that disorganized and famine-ravaged country the task was naturally difficult, but believers received help from foreign brethren in the faith, who also in another way had made a contribution to the rebuilding of society. In the German prison camps for Russian war prisoners, believing Russian soldiers had formed Bible groups among themselves. This evangelistic work was supported and furthered particularly by the Baptists but also by others. In this way not only were many soldiers baptized but hundreds of them were trained to become evangelists. After their return home they were able to strengthen this program all the more. Obviously, there existed a great need for such support. The congregations seldom if ever had paid ministers at that time. They did have paid evangelists who worked for one month at a time in the home congregation and for two months elsewhere. Bible schools to train evangelists and pastors were established. In 1924 a Bible school was opened by the Evangelical Christians in Leningrad for the training of presbyters (elders), as the leaders came to be called; and the Baptists began a "preachers' " school in Moscow in 1927.

There were nine congregations of Evangelical Christians in Leningrad and six in Moscow. But in almost all the larger and smaller cities as well as in a large number of villages, wrote Prochanov, congregations could be found. Amman, in his book on the history of the Russian church,[60] tells us that many in the confusion of those stirring times sought comfort and certainty among the Baptists, who rallied a large following. It is a fact that many, particularly among the young, turned to the Evangelical Christians and Baptists. It was impossible to organize a national youth movement, for that right was reserved exclusively for the League of Young Communists. But in every congregation there were young people's groups which actively devoted themselves to various campaigns among the youth and promoted a new lifestyle without tobacco or alcohol, opposed the coarsening of morals and were concerned about the spiritual and moral education of the youth. Among the working youth these groups had a considerable following.

Besides the active distribution of Bibles and spiritual literature and the building up of congregations, one of the most remarkable phenomena of those twenty years, the founding of Christian farm settlements, must be mentioned. The Christian collective farms, much like the kibbutzim of Israel, soared in popularity in those years. The Evangelical Christians and the Baptists were among a number of other groups that had similar settlements, often of immense proportions. The best known were probably the two Evangelical Christian communes in the vicinity of

Kalinin, called Bethany and Gethsemane. They each received support from the state because of their contribution to the economy. These farms brought into actual practice a form of Christian communism. Personal ownership was abolished, not by state law, but from inner conviction and, very likely, from an old Russian communal tradition; thus they sought new forms of the Christian communal life depicted in Acts 2: 41-47. Prochanov speaks of a work congregation and mentions the influence it exerted. "Let your light so shine before men that they may see your good works and glorify your Father which is in heaven" (Matt. 5: 16), he writes, and adds, "The light is already shining, but it will shine in much larger circles." That was the big mistake of Prochanov and others with him. Naturally they used the time allotted them in the best possible way, but they judged the immediate future too optimistically. Soon the policies of the Soviet authorities would take a fatal turn, but for the present they still had a chance for growth which they did not fail to take advantage of.

I. S. Prochanov was certainly the most characteristic and influential figure among the Russian Protestants in those twenty years. His dynamic guidance was noticeable in every sector of the life of the church. But his vision embraced even more. The evangelical movement wanted to create a church of converted and born-again people who regulated their lives according to the dictates of the Gospel. But the goal is not only, writes Prochanov, a church reform in the historical sense of that word but the regeneration of all of society. This was the goal they were to work for. At the congress of the Federation of Evangelical Christians held in Leningrad in 1926, after a report by Prochanov, it was resolved that they would dedicate themselves, in the midst of the Russian people, to a new lifestyle founded on the Gospel. Not only the conversion of people but the penetration of all sectors of human life with the spirit of the Gospel: that must be the goal. A bold plan and a grand conception! Remarkable that a group coming out of persecution and an oppressed minority position was now capable of developing such a broad vision of church and society. It would appear that the pietistic roots had not produced a narrow-minded, introverted mentality but an awakened Christianity with a strong sense of calling with respect to social problems. The development of science and art were included in this broad vision. "At least half of the students in the Academy of Sciences must consist of Evangelical Christians," writes Prochanov. But the original purity and simplicity was, of course, to be preserved. In business and profession, the Evangelical Christian was, quite artlessly, to attract attention by his love for his work and by his zealous fulfillment of duty. The idea is stressed that salvation is not only a matter of the personal salvation experience of the believer but also of the new life in Christ, the Risen Lord, the Omnipotent who rules all things. The rich tradition of the Orthodox faith also lies at the very foundation of this vision of the Evangelical Christians. It is clear, therefore, that they should not be thought of as an imported sect but as standing in the spiritual tradition of their own people. The boldest plan of all, one barely begun, was Prochanov's scheme to build a city where people might live as brothers and sisters according to Biblical guidelines. The city was to be named Evangelsk or Sun City. With permission from the Ministry of Agriculture a location in Siberia was selected and on September 11, 1927, the first oak trees were planted in the presence of the local Soviet authorities. But soon opposition to the building of a Christian city developed in Communist circles, which soon caused the plan to shipwreck. Prochanov and his followers never got any further than the planting of oak trees.

That the Evangelical Christians wanted to be a

Russian reform movement was demonstrated by the evangelic appeal made by Prochanov to the Orthodox Church, particularly to the progressive groups within that church, in 1922. A schism had developed in the Orthodox Church in those years. A group of priests who had received some support from the new regime had convened a church synod during the imprisonment of Patriarch Tikhon. They wanted to reform the church, limit the authority of the bishop, give greater responsibility to the laity, and permit a freer interpretation of dogma. At the same time they wanted to meet the new regime positively. One of the leading figures was the metropolitan Antonin of Moscow, inspirer of a group calling itself "the renaissance of the church." This reform movement was influenced by Protestant ideas and may not be identified solely with a "Red" church. Other motives besides political played a role. Prochanov addressed them in the name of the All-Russian Federation of Evangelical Christians, offering, on behalf of the believers who had been persecuted in the church for so many years, forgiveness in the name of Christ. Further, he challenged the living powers within the Russian church "to build again the tabernacle of David which is fallen down" and to carry through a real evangelical reform. Moreover, he expressed the wish to help them in this by meeting in prayer together. Different meetings of this nature were held. Metropolitan Antonin in particular took a very positive stand toward the Evangelical Christians and placed his church in Moscow at their disposal. Once, when visiting with Prochanov, the metropolitan took a little book out of his cabinet and said, "In that book I find daily food for my soul." It was the hymn book *The Harp* compiled by Prochanov. But this time of fraternity was to be only a short interlude. The conservative Orthodox side fiercely rejected contact with the Evangelical Christians and other "sectarians," and Prochanov himself, though these contacts, got himself into serious difficulties with the state police. After this short period, communication between Orthodox and Evangelical Christians and Baptists never really got started again. Communication in those years was also criticized because one of the parties engaged in it was itself divided, embroiled in a conflict with the patriarchal leadership at a time when the latter was being persecuted. It became clear that the Communist regime was not going to betray its anti-religious character, nor allow the Evangelical Christians and Baptists freedom to grow and develop independently. At first, in 1919, the Soviets had embraced in their law the right to refuse military service and choose alternative service instead. For the Mennonites, Molokani, Tolstoyites, and many Evangelical Christians and Baptists who harbored pacifist ideas, this meant quite a concession. But already in 1923 this privilege was revoked because too many made use of it. Prochanov was imprisoned and forced to urge Evangelical Christians to fulfill their military service. On the 12th of August, 1923, he wrote a letter to all the congregations on behalf of the Council of Evangelical Christians, in which he called upon believers to fulfill faithfully all the duties the state laid upon them.[61]

> The Evangelical Christians under the old regime fought for freedom of conscience with the means Christ allotted them, just as the Soviet government is doing now with worldly means. We urge all our brethren to co-operate honestly and in complete obedience in all Soviet military and civic institutions and not to refuse military service in the Red army.

Even though the Federation of Evangelical Christians was built along strict democratic principles, the influence of Prochanov's personality was unusually great. The federation was led by a conference of delegates who annually elected the members of the council of the federation, which was assigned an executive task. There were about seventy districts with district councils and district conferences. All appointees, even in the congregations, had to be chosen anew annually. After 1944 in the new Union of Evangelical Christians and Baptists we shall rediscover the same structure in principle, even though the democratic principle of executives chosen by a conference was initially less clearly established. The influence of the Evangelical Christians on the organization of the Union is clear. Walter Birnbaum[62] sees in this one of their marks. Originally they came from the Alliance Congregation in St. Petersburg in which believers from various churches had joined together. The Orthodox element, however, was the most important in the long run, and they brought with them a deep sense of true catholicity, or as it is called in Russian, *sobornost*. They were interested in the whole, the wholeness of the body of Christ. Prochanov, himself coming from the Molokani, demonstrated that in his dealings with the reform movement within Orthodoxy. "We don't want to be a sect, we want to become *church*," he once remarked at a conference in Hamburg. Among the Stundists so strongly influenced by the Baptists, the individualistic principle was dominant and the believer's baptism of the individual was central. In the Baptist movement it is generally more difficult to achieve integrated ecclesiastical structures. Many national unions of individual congregations, particularly in Anglo-Saxon countries, originated relatively late. The German as well as the Russian Baptists, unlike their English-speaking brethren, have tried from the beginning to achieve a federation or union of congregations. Nonetheless, the individualistic principle dominated, a fact which often helps evangelism but which seldom leads to broader church formation. Whether this characterization is entirely correct is difficult to judge. The fact is that in the period of the twenty years, the two most important Protestant currents, the Evangelical Christians and the Baptists, were not able to arrive at a unity. Attempts toward unity were made repeatedly and many conversations took place between 1912 and 1921 to effectuate such a union. But differences in origin and views have precluded success. The beginnings of each group were different, and each initially found adherents among people of a different social atmosphere. Other factors also contributed, such as differing notions of baptism and the Lord's Supper, induction into ministerial office, and the guidance of the congregations, all of which can perhaps best be understood in terms of an antithesis between "open" and "closed" Baptist groups. Moreover, the forming of an independent union of Evangelical Christians was not fully understood by the Baptists nor did they always approve of congregations joining that union which, in their judgment, belonged with them. A complex interplay of factors kept the two groups separated. Very likely there were also personal motives: the powerful and somewhat authoritarian personality of Prochanov made a complete union less attractive for the Baptists, who themselves had such strong leaders as Pavlov and Masayev.

But soon these problems would be overshadowed by a much greater problem. The difficulties of this time of relative freedom are of an entirely different nature than the worries which had to be faced in 1929. Suddenly it became a question of survival. In 1928 Prochanov had taken part in a world congress of Baptists held in Toronto. On his way back news reached him that new persecutions of Evangelical Christians and Baptists had broken out. He remained in the West where, in 1935, he died in Berlin. In the fatherland the Evangelical Christians and Baptists now experienced one of the most grievous periods in their history. How abruptly this came about is shown by the fact that the secretary of the union of Baptist congregations, who also visited the congress in Toronto, had presented there a most optimistic picture of religious freedom in Russia. A few weeks after his return he was arrested and exiled to central Asia.

In 1929 Stalin decided that all agriculture would be forced to collectivize. The farmlands must be converted into *kolkhozen,* collective farms. The *kulaks,* the independent farmers, must disappear. The Evangelical Christians and Baptists belonged largely to the farming classes—most of them had become prosperous through their industry and simplicity—and to the independent tradesmen and small businessmen in the cities. These social groups were precisely the ones hardest hit by Stalin's new measures. The rapidly rising influence of these "sectarians," particularly among the young, and their strong social activity, made the government decide to deal especially with them. On April 8, 1929, a new law dealing with religious fellowships was issued.[63] A religious society was defined as a local association of believing citizens, over eighteen years of age, consisting of at least twenty members. These groups were supposed to apply for registration and for acknowledgment by the authorities. They were forbidden to collect funds for mutual aid and associations of producers or co-operatives; to provide for their fellow members any form of material help; and to organize religious and other meetings, especially for children and young men and women—whether they concerned the Bible, literature, or some other theme was immaterial, or whether they practiced sewing, manual labor, or religious instruction. Further, it was forbidden to organize excursions and to maintain playgrounds for children, and to establish libraries, reading rooms, sanatoriums, and other medical services. In buildings and areas designated for religious services, only such books might be kept which were required for the specific religious service in question. The work area of religious workers, preachers, and ministers was restricted to the place where the church was located and where the members of the fellowship lived. From this summary we receive an excellent description of the activities of the Evangelical Christians and Baptists in the 20's of this century, for everything forbidden here belonged to the work of these groups. We can also better understand how heavy the blows fell. John Shelton Curtiss[64] says in his book about the church in the Soviet Union, which deals only with the Orthodox Church, that many of these restrictions were more detrimental to the rapidly growing "sectarians of Protestant character" than to the Orthodox Church, which seldom bothered about nonreligious activities and which was more conventional in its organization. Moreover, he quotes the opinion of an American theologian who was in Russia at that time and who was supposedly informed by a prominent personality, that the above-mentioned restrictions, summed up in article 17 of the decree, were included at the insistence of an Orthodox priest. It seems that this man had formerly worked among the sectarians as a missionary and now felt obliged to alert the authorities that the law favored the sects too much. It is not the only accusation one meets in the history of the church under the Soviet regime. I think that we must be extremely careful with such reports; they are often inspired by the desire to discredit the Christians. The result of the 1929 decree was that the activities of the Evangelical Christians and Baptists were limited to church worship services. Printing and distributing Bibles and other literature had to stop. Magazines were not allowed to appear any more, and training schools were closed. Evangelism could be carried on only through personal contacts; any activity at the national level was made impossible by the restrictions on the activities of the leaders. The last congresses of the Evangelical Christians and of the Baptists were held in 1930. The years following 1929, especially 1936 and 1937, were extremely grave, with numerous arrests, convictions, and banishments. The downfall of the prosperous independent farmers and the lower middle classes affected many believers. Not only did they suffer through this catastrophe, they also became victims of a direct persecution in 1937. The congregations were decimated, and only a steadfast core remained.

The revolution of 1917 affected the German Lutheran congregations and the Mennonites in an entirely different way. Because of the 1918 law requiring the separation of church and state and church and school, the bonds between the state and the Evangelical Lutheran Church in Russia were completely broken.[65] The church regulation of 1832 was annulled, state support stopped, and church officials were thrown into desperate financial circumstances, the more so now that their parsonages became state property and they had to leave them. A temporary church order was drawn up in which the independence of the local congregation was established. In the beginning of the twenty-year period, church life gradually revived and the more liberal New Economic Policy (NEP) was affirmed in the granting of permission to call a general synod of the Lutheran churches. In June, 1924, for the first time since the beginning of the Lutheran Church in Russia, delegates of congregations from all over the country convened in Moscow in order mutually to deliberate upon the life of their church and to draw up a new church regulation. In a message to the Soviet government they expressed their gratitude that this synod could be held. It was due to the separation of church and state and the resultant equality of treatment of all the churches that this convocation was made possible. Moreover, they promised the authorities complete loyalty :

> The confession of the Evangelical Lutheran Church obligates each citizen of the state belonging to this church to respect the authorities and

the existing legislation; to obey the orders of the government and to follow all duties laid upon the citizens, including military service. Thus, the people who confess to believe the Evangelical Lutheran faith have always been loyal and will continue to be so.

It seemed as if the old policy of peaceful loyalty could be continued without too much trouble. "New life can bloom out of ruins," said Bishop A. Malmgren, one of the most important figures in this period, along with the bishops Th. Meyer and O. Palsa. Bishop Palsa represented the church management of Finnish, Latvian, and Estonian congregations. On a trip through Siberia Bishop Meyer was able to reorganize the life of the congregations. In 1925 a seminary for the training of ministers was opened in Leningrad. After the Baltic countries became independent, new theologians were no longer permitted to come from Dorpat. At that time there was still eighty-two ministers in active service (in 1917, a hundred) for the approximately 1.3 million Lutherans.

In the large congregations of Moscow and Leningrad and in the Volga colony lay the center of gravity of church life. Many there had to drift along on their own resources and the sexton played an important role in congregational life. A heavy responsibility came to rest on the church members themselves; it was now possible to get a sound indication of how far the old principle of the general priesthood of believers went in actual practice. Apparently it did not succeed in every respect and the difficulties were many. Revival came about very laboriously. Indeed, there was hardly sufficient time for it, because after 1929 the situation especially for rural congregations grew progressively more difficult.

In 1933 one more general synod was convened and the last seven students from the seminary were inducted into office. Soon after that, however, a general decay of

101

church life set in. There were but eight active ministers in the whole country in 1936; the rest were imprisoned or exiled, or forbidden to exercise any function of their office. Religious instruction was no longer possible, and only in the family could religious life be perpetuated. In 1938 Peter and Paul Church in Moscow was closed, the last church to remain open.

The history of the Mennonites in that period differs little from that of the Lutheran colonists. In 1925 - 1926 some of them saw an opportunity to emigrate to Canada. The greater part of them, however, remained in Russia and shared the fate of the other believers. In order to escape from the pressure exerted on the German colonists and from administrative inclusion in the German national districts formed by the Soviet government, they formed an organization which they called "The Association of Citizens of Dutch Descent in the Ukraine."[66] Thus they sought to keep their identity. Far from succeeding, they too became the victims of religious persecutions in the next thirty years. The war, finally, scattered them everywhere.

VIII. A New Beginning

After the invasion of Russia by the German armies on June 22, 1941, the attitude of the Soviet government toward the church began to change quite rapidly. It was now necessary to mobilize all energies in the fatherland's battle against the foreign usurper. That part of the citizenry which was still religious had to be encouraged to regard the war as a national emergency they could share in meeting, while a tendency to regard the invader as a liberator had to be discouraged at all costs. There was, however, not the slightest danger of that among the bishops of the Orthodox Church. Immediately after the German invasion, Metropolitan Sergii sent a message to all Orthodox priests, reminding them of the patriotism of the forefathers and closing with these words: "The Church of Christ blesses all believers in the defense of the holy ground of our fatherland."

Already in June, 1941, all anti-religious propaganda was suspended, the magazine of the Union of the Godless no longer appeared, and anti-religious museums were closed. The church once more received a little more room to move; thus, for example, in Moscow on Easter, 1942, the rule forbidding believers to leave the house on that night was suspended to permit the faithful the opportunity to attend midnight masses. In September, 1943, Stalin received some bishops, and permission to choose a patriarch was granted. Metropolitan Sergii was thus elected. A new harmony developed between church and authorities, and a church excelling in patriotism, one that was adept at playing a role to secure better relations with foreign countries, could now emerge from the catacombs. This was literally true for various leaders of the Evangelical Christians and Baptists. They too could profit by the changed attitude of the authorities and could organize themselves anew. Various leaders were released from prisons to take their former places. They too supported Soviet patriotism and in 1942 made an appeal to the Baptists of the world, in which they claimed to speak for many believers. In order to regulate attitudes between church and state, a state committee was formed in October, 1943, to oversee the affairs of the Orthodox Church. Heading this committee was G. G. Karpov. A similar committee was formed for other religious groups, including Protestants, under the leadership of I. Polyanski. In 1966 these two committees were merged into a Council for Religious Affairs charged with seeing to it that laws regarding church life were carried out. Naturally, this committee had extensive control and great influence. In this way the Soviet authorities attempted to keep an eye on religious life as well as to carefully follow church development and possibly to regulate it. One can see a parallel in the mandate the procurator was given by the synod of the czarist Orthodox Church. The influence of the state committee for religious affairs had also contributed toward bringing together the various Protestant groups within one ecclesiastical union. There was, as we have seen, an attempt made already in 1884 to get the two main currents of the Evangelical Christians and Baptists to flow together in one common stream. Neither then nor later did the two closely allied groups succeed in coming to organizational unity.

There were, naturally, close relations; moreover, a common lot bound them together. The Evangelical Christians had succeeded somewhat better than the Baptists in maintaining themselves during the persecutions. Perhaps they were considered more of a Russian "sect" than the Baptists, who could be more easily identified with strange foreign groups. Accordingly, the Evangelical Christians had been able to show Christian concern for the Baptists in Moscow and in other places as well. In 1936 the Baptist congregation in Moscow was forced to dissolve, but the Evangelical Christians were able to continue to hold their meetings and had a former Reformed church on the *Malvi Vusovski Periulok* (Little Vusovski St.) at their disposal. The building is today the Moscow Center. But organized church life after 1929 fell into rapid decay. Serge Bolshakoff[67] writes that of the 3,219 congregations in Russia in 1928, only 1,000 were left in 1940. Thus a new awakening was necessary, and the changed attitude of the regime provided the possibility. From October 26 through 29, 1944, the delegates of the Evangelical Christians and Baptists met in Moscow and founded the Union of Evangelical Christians and Baptists. One must consider this meeting the beginning of a new unity which, however, still had to prove itself in actual practice. In judging the new structures, we shall have to keep in mind that we are discussing here a union of congregations. The Baptist conception of the church has its starting point in the independence of the local congregation which unites itself with other congregations in a federation or union. The Russian Baptist, however, has always emphasized the union concept more strongly and absolute local autonomy less strongly than Baptists elsewhere. The Union of Evangelical Christians and Baptists has the basic structure of a federation. The joining of other groups is consequently easier. This structure, however, was intersected in a remarkable way by a sort of hidden hierarchical principle whereby, as a result of the influence of the authorities, a position of leadership was created which was difficult to reconcile with Baptist principle. The difficulties of the revision of the ecclesiastical statutes that were to lead to a schism in the 60's find their origin in part right here. In a letter to Khrushchev (August 13, 1963) a group complaining of the leadership of the Evangelical Christians and Baptists writes : [68]

> In the war years (1943 - 44) the Council for the Affairs of Religious Cults, bound to the Council of Ministers of the U.S.S.R., was created, and this body is now the special supreme authority over the church. At the same time the All-Union Council of the Evangelical Christians/Baptists was created to be a leading body. This council was not elected by the church, but was brought into being by the state authorities and consisted principally of churchmen who had consented to deviate from the evangelical doctrine and agreed to an illegal collaboration with various state authorities. To that end some of them were released from detention before their terms were up.

It is a somewhat one-sided and colored image which is given us here of the leading persons in the newly-founded union. They were accused of departing from the evangelical doctrine of the independence of the local congregations. To suggest, however, that the new leaders of the Union, some of whom had come directly from prison where they had landed because of their religious convictions and steadfastness, were now committed to betray the Gospel, is an unjust imputation. On the contrary, they saw in the changed attitude of the Soviet state a possibility to rebuild church life and could not do otherwise than accept the possibilities, limited though they were, that

106

were given them. It is true that the structure of the Union, and in particular the way in which the governing body was established, was somewhat obscure. The statutes of 1944 and 1948 were never published. The statutes of 1963 (amended in 1966) presently in force are well known and demonstrate considerable growth in democratic principles. The Union is led by the Union Council, which is now chosen by a congress of delegates. This was formerly not the case, and the Union Council had an almost unassailable position, since the same members continued to hold the office of leadership. We may not, however, suggest that the leadership of 1944 consisted of arbitrary figures which the state had dredged up out of the darkness.

Yacob Zhidkov, the first president of the Union Council (he died in 1966 shortly after his retirement from office), was already chairman for some twenty years of the Union of Evangelical Christians. A. V. Karev also (died November 24, 1971), the secretary-general, was one of the leading figures of the Evangelical Christians. The Union Council nominated seventy senior presbyters, all reliable men, who were entrusted with the care of the church in the various republics and districts of Russia. The Soviet Union was divided into seventy districts, and each district had appointed to it one senior presbyter. They function in the name of the Union Council to which they are responsible for their actions. Their task is especially to assist the lay preachers in their work in the congregations. One can best compare them to the superintendents in the German Lutheran churches. Thus there was clearly in the union structure a line from above to below. Almost from the very beginning there were objections to this arrangement which bore a sort of unofficial hierarchical structure. Viewed historically, this structure is easily explicable when we think of the church order of the Lutheran Church in czarist Russia, where there had also been a strong central ecclesiastical government. It is not so strange that in the regulating of the new ecclesiastical organization there should be a reaching back to the models of czarist times. Even an atheistic government would tend to do that. Since Peter the Great the state had been mixed up in the life of the church, and it was undoubtedly difficult to imagine that it could be otherwise. Examples of a "free" church in Russian history are hardly to be found. A strong, central, co-ordinated agency one could justly advocate, even from the standpoint of the church, in a country so big and with so many scattered and often small groups. Among the Evangelical Christians/ Baptists, however, there is no natural tendency to seek or to accept supervision and directive care by the state. The tendency of the authorities to keep a very watchful eye on the development of church life was emphasized in the stipulation that each congregation of more than twenty persons must request registration from the local Soviet authorities. This request would then be sent on to higher officials and finally the decision regarding acknowledgment would be lodged with the Council for Religious Affairs. The registration can be refused if the members of the fellowship do not acknowledge Soviet regulation regarding the churches and in their doctrine and liturgy incite the believers to break the law and established order. An element of arbitrariness is undoubtedly present in the acknowledgment of religious communities. In letters of protest it has been stated that only in one definite period (1947 - 1948) were registrations of Evangelical Christian/ Baptist congregations accepted. In an October, 1961, letter to Khrushchev from the Baptist congregation in Vladivostok, it was said: [69]

> Here the principle of freedom of conscience and religion has been grossly violated. There is not a single registered community in the region. We are all forced to assemble without registration, although we have asked for it repeatedly and

insistently. There is not a single community where the police functionaries have not appeared with threats to prohibit church services.

Many fellowships seem to have been forced in this way to lead an illegal existence with all its miserable consequences. According to some reports, two-thirds of the existing communities have supposedly not received recognition. The accuracy of these reports can, naturally, be checked by no one. Very likely, a number have not even requested registration because they objected to interference by the state and preferred a sort of underground existence.

It is therefore very difficult to get any idea of how great the number of Evangelical Christians/Baptists is. The number of 500,000 confessing members is generally suggested. We must remember, however, that only baptized adults are included in this figure. The fellowship must be considerably larger when one includes family members and sympathizers. But the strength of the Evangelical Christians/Baptists does not lie in statistics and membership registers. In a country where it can cause problems for education and career to belong to a church and in which one is inclined to keep one's inner life to himself, it is even more difficult to measure in statistics the actual extensiveness of a congregation's influence. One can, however, point to the spreading of the Evangelical Christian/Baptist congregations throughout the whole Russian empire. In European Russia many congregations exist in the old districts of the southern Ukraine and the Caucasus and also in the Baltic republics. In Estonia are eighty-three congregations. On April 26, 1970, in the St. Olai Church of Tallinn, a new senior presbyter was installed in the presence of 2,000 believers. But especially in Asiatic Russia the number of congregations has increased. Often they are of considerable proportions. Because the church buildings are small and paper members do not exist, every visitor from Western countries (where church attendance often is not very impressive) is struck by the lively atmosphere and crowded services. To be a church member means to be an involved church member. In a country where the general atmosphere is not just indifferent but often hostile to ecclesiastical and religious life, and in a church with no tradition of bourgeois adjustment but only of suffering and oppression, the members are naturally only those who are truly involved in the life of the church. The worship services are led by the pastors, but they are not the only ones who preach. The lay preachers also give their testimony, and the service, which by our standards lasts a long time, from two to three hours, often consists of three meditations. Depending on the makeup and spiritual background of the congregation, the service can seem overly emotional to us. Of course, one must take into consideration the pressure under which the believers often live and the emotional need to express themselves in the fellowship of like-minded believers. They are completely involved. But it is also possible that the influence of certain groups standing in an old Russian tradition is responsible for less stress on preaching and more on the Spirit-filled intimate atmosphere created in part by singing. Evening services are held during the week; other kinds of congregational meetings are not permitted. In Russia religious freedom means only the limited freedom of a liturgical service. This satisfies the Orthodox Church more than the Evangelical Christians and Baptists, but as a result of such government regulation the emphasis for them has also fallen more on church services, and it is in the services that the life of the church expresses itself. The people sing slowly, stirringly, and frequently. There is not a congregation which does not have a choir that sings regularly in the service. The hymns, according to Prochanov, must be a harmonious fusion of evangelical joy and popular melancholy. Church hymns from the

Western Protestant world have been translated, especially the revival hymns from the second half of the last century and later. There are, however, also hymns from their own still-brief history. Hymnbooks are to be had only in limited numbers. Many church members, accordingly, have copied the hymns in notebooks. In a description of the work of the Evangelical Christians/Baptists in a Communist magazine[70] we read :

> The purpose of choir-singing in the worship services is to create an atmosphere of reverence among the believers. In the hymns motifs from familiar Soviet and folk songs are often used, which are for the most part poetic. In order to attract the young people, the members of these denominations organize c h o i r s and music ensembles whereby they take advantage of our poor cultural efforts in some districts. And they organize get-acquainted meetings and family socials where sermons on religious life are read. The groups also celebrate Soviet holidays, such as conducting May Day excursions ... the members of these sects strongly emphasize personal contacts. Someone who has experienced adversity in his life is shown sympathetic understanding and thus is influenced to join the group.

Other publications often point out how these groups frequently turn to the forgotten folk in society. Naturally, this practice is described in Communist publications as an objectionable form of proselytism. On the contrary, we must regard it as a positive expression of social concern and as the only way in which they can give expression to it. The lonely, widows, invalids, old people, folk who have no place in a society in which labor and development are central, these often find their only support in the believers who in practice also want to testify to the love of Christ.

To own a Bible is not a matter of course for the believer in the Soviet Union. The printing of a small number of Bibles and hymnbooks was permitted in 1953 after Stalin's death, but the demand remains much larger than the supply. After 1958 when Khrushchev began to impose restrictions on church life, the printing of Bibles was out of the question. Only the church paper *Bratskii Vestnik* (News of the Brethren) might still appear six times a year. Not until 1968 was permission granted to print 25,000 hymnbooks and 20,000 Bibles. A congregation of some 400 members was apportioned, for example, twenty Bibles. A Bible remains a precious possession in the Soviet Union. Foreigners visiting a church service can count on being asked if by any chance they have a Russian Bible. On the whole it is extremely difficult to acquire Christian theological literature.

Bourdeaux[71] confirms my own observation that the pastors have only a small library at their disposal and that the public libraries naturally have little to offer in their particular field. In the bookcase of a young minister he found a copy of the Bible, two pre-Revolution books on Christian doctrine and the history of the Orthodox Church, and an English paperback on the office of healing. It is not easy to have so little to fall back on when one must lead in public worship so often. Moreover, they cannot depend on help from colleagues since they are so isolated and the congregations are so distant from each other. Little imagination is needed to realize that one can persevere in such practice only if the congregation is a real fellowship, a core church gathered round the Bible in meditation and prayer. Without idealizing it, one naturally thinks of the situation of some congregations in apostolic times.

The training of ministers is certainly one of the sore points in church life after the war. From 1956 to 1958 a few ministers studied in England. In 1968 permission was again secured for three ministers to study for two years at Spurgeon's College in London. But the lack of a home training institute is certainly one of the greatest handicaps that exists there. The hope expressed in 1946 that a training school would soon be opened has not yet become a reality. Through correspondence courses and regional meetings they tried as much as possible to supplement the training of the ministers. In 1968 a two-year Bible course for ministers was begun, the candidates being appointed by the local congregations. The monthly study material includes introduction to the Bible, exegesis, dogmatics, pastoral theology, and church history. Twice a year preliminary examinations are held in Moscow. Not more than a hundred candidates can take this course. The lack of a good theological training of a large group of ministers is keenly felt by the Evangelical Christians/Baptists. We ought to bear in mind, however, that in actual practice the ministers do not form their own separate group but are completely integrated into the fellowship and have emerged out of the rank and file of the people. For all members of the congregation in reality share in the priestly office of believers. It is through the congregations that the ministers were called to their office, and the deacons and presbyters are distinguished by the fact that they were chosen for their faith and steadfastness. Many of them work in industry and agriculture—most believers are to be found among the working population in the city and in the country, while only a small group belong to the intelligentsia—and there attract attention by their serious and dedicated attitude toward life and their positive commitment to their tasks. They abstain from the use of tobacco and alcoholic drinks. The Evangelical Christians/Baptists certainly have no negative outlook on the world. The positive attitude expressed in their various callings and preaching which leans heavily toward personal sanctification and a consciously Christian attitude toward

113

life, all attest to this. Yet there is a continuing discussion within the Christian fellowship as to what stands one ought to assume toward the cultural environment in which one is now living. This finds expression, for example, in the question on whether one can accept films and television, clubs and theaters. Of course these are completely determined by Marxist-Leninist ideology; how to accept the Soviet socio-economic order without accepting this ideology creates a problem particularly complicated for them. As a religious group they stand outside the general culture. They know that if they want to preserve their identity they shall have to resist the spiritual and cultural pressure of their environment by preserving also a certain distance. In this situation one can justly defend the proposition that there is strength in isolation. Moreover, we have already seen that men like Prochanov, with his Christian socialism in the period of the 20's, were not principally seeking cultural isolation. The believers were driven into this isolation by Soviet society, which wanted, as it were, to hide them away on the reservation of isolated church services. They have not accepted this role, however, because as believing Christians they desired to continue taking part in the life of their society, exerting their influence on it, not through public activities or evangelism campaigns in stadiums, not through radio services or personable television programs, but through personal actions and contacts with individual Soviet citizens, at funerals or weddings, when family visiting, wherever the opportunity presents itself. M. Y. Zhidkov, minister of the congregation in Moscow, stated at the August, 1969, congress of the European Baptist Federation, of which he was president, that in 1968 there were fourteen new members added to the Moscow congregation by baptism.[72] The first question asked of each candidate was: "Tell us how you came to faith in God." About half of the candidates pointed to a witness through whom

114

they first heard of God and whom they could thank that they now belonged to Christ. One candidate said : "I first met him at work. At the outset I paid attention to him because he was different from the rest, he did his work well, was modest and sober. Then one day he came to me. He often talked with me with genuine love, he was concerned about me and invited me to take part in the church services. I came, and thereafter gave my heart to God."

The Evangelical Christians/Baptists attract attention by their work ethics and performance, and not infrequently it has happened that a workman praised for his work has turned out to be a believing Baptist. One can assume, therefore, that the personal attacks often appearing in the Soviet press against the Baptists have little influence and are dismissed by serious readers. They are recognized after all as peaceful, hard-working people who distinguish themselves by their sober attitude toward life and their concern for their neighbors. Inspired by anti-religious propaganda, news reports depicting them as a social element of low caliber are, curiously enough, sometimes reprinted in Western newspapers. A Dutch newspaper passed on a report from the Russian press regarding a minister who distilled alcohol in his attic. One can hardly betray a greater misconception of what is taking place in the Soviet Union and of the character of the Evangelical Christians and Baptists. It is through their personal attitude toward life and through their personal contact with others that they are even now able to give their religious testimony. The modern Russian writer Alexander Solzhenitsyn in his book *One Day in the Life of Ivan Denisovich* writes about the behavior and attitude of a Baptist prisoner. He describes him as a calm, helpful, and patient man. His dearest possession is his little Bible and he speaks freely to his fellow prisoners about his faith. Basic to this life attitude is the conception that spiritual regeneration by the Holy Spirit, which precedes baptism, must go hand in hand with a change in disposition and behavior. Indeed, one is not lightly accepted for baptism but only after a certain preparatory period during which time one has given ample evidence of this change.

Faith and attitude toward life are bound together, and the one inspires the other. A stern puritan conception of life governs these Evangelical Christians and Baptists, who in their life and work strive after the simplicity of the early Christian church. In their conception of faith they are strictly traditional and their Biblical interpretations are fundamentalistic. W. Kahle[73] rightly observes that this is the result not merely of a lack of theologians or of the absence of "progressive" intellectuals, but especially of the way in which these congregations exist in their environment. An adjusted cultural Christianity would not endure for very long. The image they gave of themselves in a 1946 letter to their American brethren in the faith is worth borrowing at this point. They sent this letter along with a returning American visitor: [74]

Dear Brothers and Sisters in Christ!

Taking advantage of the visit to our country of our esteemed brother, Dr. Louie Newton, communion with whom has afforded us much joy and spiritual pleasure, the U.S.S.R. Council of Baptist and Evangelical Christians, in the name of all our Russian brothers and sisters, sends you a hearty and brotherly greeting. Dr. Newton has asked us to write you a letter, and it gives us great joy to comply with his request. There is much happiness in the life of our Russian Baptist brotherhood, and we feel it of value to share this happiness with you.

We should first of all note several specific features of our spiritual life and activity with which you, Baptists of the United States of America, may not be familiar, and which may somewhat distinguish our Christianity

116

from yours. There are five such distinctive features of the Christian Baptists of the U.S.S.R.

1. The Principle of Unity

Three large rivers — the Baptists, Evangelical Christians, and Pentecostals, who share the Baptist religious principles of resurrection and baptism—have fused into one mighty river whose beneficent waters now flow all over our vast country. All secondary differences which formerly, before our union, separated these three religious currents, are being smoothed out more and more in mutual understanding and brotherly love which are growing and strengthening, in the friendly harmonious work of the Kingdom of God in our beloved land. We fervently thank the Lord for being able to carry out his sacred desire— "That all may be one"—and we should like to see this wish of his for unity among his children become close and dear to all Christian churches throughout the world.

2. The Preaching of the Pure Gospel

Our entire Evangelical Baptist brotherhood maintains fundamental views. We painstakingly preserve the purity of the Evangelistic and Evangelical teaching. The cross of Calvary, the sin offering of Christ, his precious blood— such is the central theme of our dogmatics and our preaching. We seek to bring to the world the pure image of our Savior just as he is given to us in the pages of the Gospels. We emphasize the divine nature of Christ. We do not deny a single one of his miracles. We do not remove a single one of his words. The complete Gospel is our doctrine.

3. The Preaching of Sanctification

The spiritual depth, purity, and sanctity of the life of our churches and their members—this is what occupies the first place in our educational work. We do not strive for numbers, although we take joy in the conversion of every sinner. Figures interest us very little and we are not especially concerned with statistics of our members. This is a specific feature of ours, and we do not consider it a bad one. The purity of the church and the highly Christian life of its members are most important for us. It seems to us that in many countries Christianity suffers with the restless spirit of Martha. We inculcate among our members the spirit of Mary, that is, the spirit of deep, meditative Christianity, which is acquired by her stay at the feet of Christ.

4. The Spirit of Early Christianity

The simplicity of the early days of Christianity is our ideal, and we strive for it in all our life and work. We do not strive for outer gloss and noisy advertising. Most of our blessings we received not in luxurious and costly houses of prayer but in simple rooms of the Jerusalem chamber type. We see how often a departure from the simplicity of the early days of Christianity leads to spiritual death and a Laodicean spirit and that the inner life wanes in spite of the outer gloss and superficial beauty of the ritual. We pray unceasingly that our Russian Evangelical-Baptist churches may not deviate from the simplicity of early Christianity.

5. It is our principle to carry on God's work in our country with our own means.

The observance of this rule has developed in our Russian churches the spirit of selfless physical service. Our brothers and sisters have learned to sacrifice not only everything within their power but even beyond their power. In this respect our churches resemble the Macedonian churches. The generosity of our believers finds expression in large offerings which cover all the needs of the work of God in our country.

Complete Religious Freedom. We have listed all the features characteristic of the spiritual life and activity of our brotherhood, and we have complete religious freedom to carry them out day after day. We deeply respect our

118

Soviet Government which has given us this freedom and protects it from any violation whatever. In our country all churches and religions enjoy equal and complete freedom. Because of this freedom we have a flourishing spiritual life in our churches. There is a great fire that burns in the hearts of our believers. The Gospel is preached freely, and thousands of sinners repent and turn to Christ. There is not a single church of ours which does not have its conversions. We have information that during the first half of this summer already thirty thousand newly converted souls were baptized. And an equal number will be baptized during the second half of this summer.

We publish a journal *Bratskii Vestnik* [*Brotherly News*] which carries throughout the Soviet Union the news of our work and the blessings from the Lord. We are publishing the Bible, the New Testament, and books of spiritual songs. We shall continue to publish these until we have satisfied all need for this material.

A School for Preachers. We shall soon open a school to train our preachers. The Orthodox Church has anticipated us in this respect, but we shall soon catch up to it. Just as we do spiritual work, we do charitable work. Regular monthly offerings are made in all our churches for the children of soldiers who died during the war. These offerings provide large funds. Ah, if you but saw the enthusiasm of our Russian believers ! How much fire ! How much love for Christ and our fellow men, how much self-sacrifice, how much simplicity in Christ !

We are far from proud, but we sincerely wish to light the entire world with the light of Christ, and to be a model of living Christianity and the simplicity of the days of the apostles. Accept this letter of ours as fraternal news of those who love you and pray for you, your brothers and sisters in the belief in Jesus Christ, who are scattered over

119

the boundless expanses of our Soviet Union. In the name of the Union of Baptist and Evangelical Christians.

Presidium of the All-Union Council: Chairman, Y. Zhidkov; Vice-Chairmen, M. Goliaev and M. Orlov; Treasurer, P. Malin; General Secretary, A. Karev.

IX. Unity

It is striking that the preceding letter begins by emphasizing the principle of unity. The great unity that came into existence at the founding of the Union in 1944 stands in the forefront of their attention. That is understandable, for the merging of the two chief currents in Russian Protestantism, repeatedly pursued in the past, had now become a fact. A sort of federative union of congregations from different backgrounds was entered into, which other groups then joined. Perhaps one should say that other groups were joined to them, for the authorities found it difficult to control the widely scattered groups of believers and therefore presumably played a part in the formation of a centrally controlled church union. The need of the Soviet authorities to have a directing and controlling grip on all types of social relationships and unions is sufficiently known to make this intervention plausible. By making it necessary for each congregation to be registered and by recognizing only those congregations affiliated with the Union, the authorities were given ample means to exert the necessary pressure. Yet the desire for unity had always been present with many Evangelical Christians and Baptists, and what was said about this unity in their letter to their American brethren is upright and well meant.

On the last Sunday in October, the Day of Unity, the

founding of the Union is annually celebrated. Since 1944 they have struggled inwardly to hold on to the unity of faith and to deepen it. That has certainly not been an easy assignment, for the groups brought together in the Union came from very different backgrounds. This church union has not been a simple matter of course. In 1945 a segment of the Pentecostal believers, called "Christians of the Evangelical Faith," joined the Union while the rest remained outside it. Others later left because they did not feel at home there. About a third of the Pentecostal congregations remained within the Union.

To preserve unity with the Pentecostal groups, much struggle will be repeatedly necessary. At the 1966 congress A. V. Karev notes that among the Christians of the Evangelical Faith as well as among the Evangelical Christians/ Baptists there were people who had difficulty accepting one another. They are traveling together, but the way is still long. He then calls to mind the work of one of the Pentecostal ministers who, above all else, sought after a real love for Christ and not so much after spiritual gifts, as if these had a worthiness in themselves. Continuing in that spirit, true unity will become possible. In 1967 a dialogue occurred between the presidium of the Union Council and the representatives of those Pentecostal congregations belonging to the Union, particularly those from the Ukraine and White Russia. They came to the conclusion that measures from both sides had to be taken to strengthen the unity and brotherly relations existing between the groups, in the interest of promoting a most fruitful common task. In the magazine *Bratskii Vestnik* there are repeated reports on the problems of achieving unity and the conversations that took place.[75]

In the local congregations where the groups have really been forced to meet, specific problems arise, as would be expected. The years 1953 and 1954 saw the return to their congregations of many prisoners and exiled who had not taken part in the difficult and complicated work of reuniting the three separated groups and had kept their negative points of view about such co-operation between the Evangelical Christians/Baptists and the Pentecostal groups. They then began to form their own groups, for example, the "Pure Baptists" and "Evangelical Christian Perfectionists."[76] The "Pure Baptists" gained influence particularly in the congregations of the Ukraine. They condemned the unity which had been achieved as impure and taught that all members must be installed into their ministry of believers by the laying on of hands. They also insisted on a more active religious propaganda and demanded the abolition of the rule that only officially chosen presbyters might conduct worship services. The splitting off of different congregations could indeed be remedied, but many of these splinter groups no doubt joined themselves to the Initsiativniki later in the 60's. Other small groups also joined the Union, such as, in 1947, the "Free Christians" who came from areas added to the Soviet Union after the war. For them, joining the Union was the only way they could continue to exist, even though they rejected even baptism and the Lord's Supper.

A factor of great importance for the growth of spiritual life within the Union was the joining of a group of Mennonites in 1963. The Mennonites in the war years had suffered the fate of the German immigrants. Though they lived in Russia for a long time, as elements dangerous to the state they were deported from their colonies to regions farther east. This effort was cut short by the rapid invasion of the German armies, and many of them joined the retreating Germans in 1943; only a small number after the war found new beginnings in Canada and Paraguay. On the way many perished or were recaptured by the Russian troops and transported to Siberia. In Asiatic Russia the survivors found new places to live, sometimes in groups together but more often as families scattered

123

among the other inhabitants. Karaganda is the largest center. In 1955 a general amnesty was announced for all Russian "Germans"; henceforth those who had been forced to live in their own country as exiles without any rights were free to live anywhere in the Soviet Union and rebuild their own social life. The number of Mennonites has been estimated at about 50,000. They are divided into two currents: the so-called "Church Mennonites" who have clung to baptism by sprinkling, and the "Mennonite Brethren" who in the preceding century had come under the influence of the Baptists and had accepted baptism by immersion. The latter, amounting to about 18,000, joined the Union of Evangelical Christians/Baptists in 1963. The old relationship with the Baptists made this fusion a matter of course. In places where no separate Mennonite fellowship existed they were incorporated into existing Evangelical Christian/Baptist fellowships. The Mennonite congregations, however, have kept their own structure, as did the Pentecostal congregations. They were incorporated into the Union of Evangelical Christians/Baptists as groups having a character all their own and could continue to use the German language as well as their own hymnals. The federative character of the Union is hereby once more clearly illustrated. The Mennonites also have their own representation in the Union Council. In 1967, at a conference of delegates of the Union Council in which seventeen delegates from the Mennonite Brethren participated, it was established that an independent congregation of Mennonite Brethren should be organized in Karaganda in addition to the congregation of Evangelical Christians/Baptists, but that the majority wanted to remain affiliated with the Union.

In another mixed congregation of Evangelical Christians/Baptists and Mennonites, serious problems had arisen about the celebration of Easter. Russian Protestants have generally followed the Julian calendar, and thus have celebrated the Christian holy days at the same time as the Orthodox. In Lutheran and Baptist circles, however, the bond with Western churches was often affirmed by their clinging to the Western Gregorian feast days. The problems of unity among Christians with their long history have often been particularly complicated. The conference wisely determined that all congregations would be free in the choice of dates for the celebration of church festival days. Concerning the Church Mennonites who do not belong to the Union, the following has been decided: [77]

> Depending upon their spiritual growth and Christian life, the Church Mennonites are permitted to preach in our congregations and to sing in our choirs. If, however, on occasion, the members of our congregation are offended by their participation in the Lord's Supper, then they are permitted to observe Holy Communion in our churches separately.

Thus they seem to have the right of guests in the congregations of the Union of Evangelical Christians and Baptists.

The Lutherans also, after the rehabilitation of the German-speaking minority, have been able to move about freely. Driven out of their original settlements, they landed mostly in the eastern territories of the Soviet Union, in Siberia and central Asia. In Kazakhstan and Alma-Ata independent Lutheran congregations soon sprang up after 1955.[78] In an eyewitness account of the first improvised meeting of a group of Lutherans in the years 1956 - 1957, we are told that they met in a barn and that the service lasted from nine o'clock in the morning to four o'clock in the afternoon. Many were baptized and confirmed. Marriages were solemnized. After twenty-five years this was once more possible. There were families in which all the children were baptized, the older children were confirmed, and the marriage of the parents was ecclesiastically blessed, all in the same service.[79] Many Lutherans have found a spiritual home with Evangelical Christians and Baptists. On the lists of imprisoned Evangelical Christians and Baptists that have lately been published in the West, German names keep recurring. In various Evangelical Christian and Baptist congregations the opportunity is given to hold meetings where the German language is used in preaching and singing. But according to recent reports, there is a clear attempt to form distinctly Lutheran groups. Some seventeen congregations are known to have received official recognition from the local authorities. Besides, there are many unofficial, unregistered groups. A farmer who in 1930 had been exiled from the territory around Odessa became a minister in a German Lutheran parish after the war. In 1965 he wrote to a woman who for many years had been a member of his congregation and who had received permission to visit her son in Württemberg. She had sent him a postcard of a Lutheran church in Württemberg.

> May God be merciful to me and allow me to enter such a house just once more and may the bells ring and the organ play above my head. But it will not happen anymore... It gives me heartfelt joy that this gift is given to you and that you can go in and out each time the bells call you, without fear, erect before God and man, and not as we.

After thirty years of exile in one's own country, this letter expresses the homesickness and longing of many. A forgotten group, these Protestant Russians of German tongue and descent. To have official ecclesiastical contact with them is not yet possible.[80]

In a travel account of a few Lutherans from West Berlin in 1969, a story is told about a visit to a Lutheran congregation in Novosibirsk :

We visited a German-speaking preacher from the Lutheran congregation and were received in his house. He told us about his pastoral work. During the day he is busy as a cabinetmaker and boss of a large division. In the city he is respected as a diligent and competent craftsman. Besides, he is a lay preacher of the Lutheran congregation that, because of the doctrine of baptism, separated itself from the Baptists. He told us that in Novosibirsk and its surroundings there were many such small congregations of up to 200 members. In western Siberia alone there were supposedly about 300 such Lutheran congregations with approximately 80 church buildings. In the mid-Asiatic republics such Lutheran congregations can also be found.

How many of the approximately 1.5 million Soviet citizens who report their nationality as German belong to a church cannot be ascertained. It seems, however, that it has been difficult for the congregations of the Evangelical Christians and Baptists to find a place for the Lutherans within their own communions. The question of adult baptism has often proved a stumbling block here.

The problem of unity remains one of the most difficult and critical for the Union of Evangelical Christians and Baptists. They are continuously busy with these questions. In 1967 A. V. Karev said : [81]

One of the most important problems of our brotherhood is the question of the unity of believers in our country. However, it must also be said that the question of unity is not only a problem of our brotherhood; it is a problem of Christendom throughout the world.

Probably the question of inner unity and co-operation is further complicated for the Union of Evangelical Christians and Baptists by the fact that different groups of

127

believers joined the Union more for the preservation of life than out of a longing for unity. In some respects the Union from its inception had a somewhat artificial and forced character. This does not apply to the two chief groups of Evangelical Christians and Baptists who since 1884 were already embarked on the road toward unity, but it does apply to other groups, where the external pressure often played a greater role than the desire for unity. The question of Christian unity is in many ways an internal church problem with the Evangelical Christians and Baptists. And with it they indeed have their hands full. In a following chapter we shall have to direct attention to the great separation that occurred after 1961, the result, as with so many past separations in the Protestant churches of Western Europe, of the relationship of church and state.

There was little possibility of contact with the Orthodox Church in the post-war era. An intensive spiritual contact does not exist, but one must reckon with the fact that the Orthodox Church has always had difficulty expressing a brotherly attitude toward those groups it considers sectarian. Among the Evangelical Christians and Baptists, moreover, there is still an uncertainty regarding the church which in the past persecuted them so. Yet the consciousness of a deeper-lying unity is clung to.

In *Bratskii Vestnik,*[82] on the occasion of the death of a believing Orthodox grandmother of a Baptist girl, one of the leaders of the Union Council had this to say:

> In every Christian church there are members of the universal church of Christ, that is to say, believers with burning hearts ... that the grand-mother shone with the light of love, gentleness, humility, and perseverance gives certain evidence that she loved Christ and therefore belonged to one universal church of Christ. The grand-

daughter and grandmother were one in regard to that important point: they both loved Christ. But the granddaughter's deeper insight on specific issues led to a different conviction, and therefore the manner of the granddaughter in worshipping God had to be different from that of the grandmother.

Here an antithetical attitude has given way to an attitude of respect for the faith of Orthodoxy and a consciousness of real unity. But of a genuine faith encounter between both fellowships no mention is made. The traditional self-consciousness of the leading circles in the Orthodox Church and the internal problems of unity experienced by the Evangelical Christians/Baptists stand in the way of such development. The points of contact between the Evangelical Christians/Baptists and the Orthodox Church lie particularly at present in the area of world peace. Since 1948 the Orthodox Church has devoted itself with unusual energy to peace propaganda. It began in Moscow when the conference of the representatives of Orthodox auto-cephalous churches called upon "the Christians of the whole world" to join them in waging an active campaign for peace. Many in the West, however, interpreted this as a sign of the subordination of the church in the Soviet Union to the state and its politics. The somewhat one-sided political orientation of this peace activity has indeed given occasion for this view. Yet it must not be forgotten that for the Russian churches a sincere will for peace is fundamental to their activities, and that there is an intense longing for peace after a war from which the Russian people suffered more than any other. It must also be remembered that only in the framework of this peace activity were they able to express the social-ethical dimensions of the faith.

Ecclesiastical delegates from Russia took part in the Peace Congress of the World Peace Council and of the

Soviet Peace Committee. In particular, Nikolai, metropolitan of Krutizi and Kolomna was one of the leading figures in the Russian peace movement. Patriarch Alexi on several occasions organized congresses for peace to which all religious groups in the Soviet Union were called to participate. The last one took place in 1969 in the monastery of Zagorsk. The Evangelical Christians/Baptists also took part in these congresses and other manifestations. Their contacts with the Orthodox Church are generally in the area of peace activities, even though their participation in those activities is much more modest. They were also involved in the Christian Peace Conferences in Prague. These were first called together in 1958 "in order to persuade the churches to devote themselves to the service of friendship, reconciliation, and peaceful co-operation among the nations." In the context of this international activity mention must yet be made of the participation of the Evangelical Christians/Baptists in the work of the Baptist World Alliance. At its 1955 congress in London, a delegation of Evangelical Christians/Baptists were present and Y. Zhidkov was elected vice president of the alliance. The Evangelical Christians/Baptists have a lively share in the work of the alliance. They also joined the World Council of Churches in 1962, as well as the Conference of European Churches, the so-called Nyborg Conference. At the time of their request for membership in the World Council, they stated that the Union counted 5,545 congregations and 545,000 members. Besides the local ministers there were 32,370 preachers in the service of the Union.[83]

X. The Initsiativniki

In the years 1954 through 1958, after the death of Stalin, there followed a short period of greater freedom of movement for the churches and believers. Police control diminished and many who had been deported could return home. But in 1969 a serious attack against the religious life was begun anew after Khrushchev became chairman of the Council of Ministers in 1958. Serious unrest developed among the party ideologists because of the increasing influence of religion on the citizens of the Soviet Union. The president of the Society for the Dissemination of Scientific and Political Knowledge declared at a congress in 1957 : "The influence of religion is still making itself felt today among an important segment of the people of the U.S.S.R. In many places the number of believers is growing. Boys and girls are falling under the influence of religion. There are Komsomols who not only admit that they are believers, but have the audacity to proclaim their faith." [84]

The anxiety of the atheistic bosses soon led to all sorts of measures to restrict the life of the churches. Particularly by stringent application of the existing legal regulations and by means of administrative measures, they tried to smother the life of the church. On August 21, 1959, *Pravda* [85] signaled the transition from the ideological to the legislative and administrative methods in this anti-religious action. The Russian Orthodox Church had a new organizational structure thrust upon the parishes, giving the local party organs greater opportunity to meddle in the life of the church. Many churches, monasteries, and seminaries were closed. The fall of Metropolitan Nikolai, well known for his participation in the party's work for peace and one of the best-known Russian bishops outside Russia, demonstrated that the authorities did not even hesitate to seize the top figures out of the shaky church establishment. The disappearance of Metropolitan Nikolai from the scene created a great stir in foreign ecclesiastical circles and gave notice of a new phase in the persecution of the church in the Soviet Union. In 1963 orthodox believers made an appeal to the "patriarchs of Jerusalem, Antioch, Constantinople, and others." In a writing that reached the West through a secret channel it was stated: [86] "Ever since 1959 the Antichrist has been busy persecuting the Orthodox Church in a most frightful way." The mandate for this had supposedly emanated from the new chairman of the Council for Russian Orthodox Church Affairs. Other reports also filtered through. In *The Times* of January 4, 1963, the following was reported: [87]

> A group of 32 Russians from an evangelical sect forced their way into the American Embassy compound today complaining of religious persecution and pleading to be sent abroad. They left nearly four hours later in a bus, some weeping bitterly, accompanied by Soviet Foreign Ministry officials. At first the group refused to enter the bus. A young man, in a black fur hat and a dark coat, said: "We don't want to go anywhere. They'll shoot us." An elderly man shouted: "There is no place in the Soviet Union for us. We demand of those people who believe

in Christ and in God, help us." The group consisted of six men, twelve women, and fourteen children. American Embassy sources said that they had made a four-day train journey from the Siberian coal mining town of Chernogorsk, more than 1,800 miles from Moscow. Some of the children appeared to be ill after the journey.

They brought with them a "small stack" of petitions complaining of religious persecution and expressing a desire to leave the Soviet Union. These were left at the embassy...

The Russians described themselves as Evangelical Christians "who regarded each other as equals and did not believe in a church hierarchy." They said they had not been allowed to hold religious services.

The people concerned with here were probably non-registered Protestants. From the documents they handed over to the embassy it appeared that their principal objections were aimed at the compulsory atheistic upbringing of their children.[88] Khrushchev's policies in regard to the churches became the direct occasion for great internal tensions and difficulties within the Union of Evangelical Christians/Baptists which we must describe in this chapter.

The conflict originated in response to the restrictive measures of the authorities. They forbade the Union Council to remain in contact with the non-registered, hence illegal, groups and congregations, and exerted great pressure on this leading organ of the Evangelical Christians/Baptists to remove the all-too-active ministers from their tasks and to dissolve churches and recombine them. Further, they wanted evangelistic activity to be limited, the number of baptisms of young people between eighteen and thirty to be reduced to a minimum, and the religious influencing of children to be avoided by keeping children of school age from attending church services.[89] These state-formulated requirements were not openly announced but were presented privately to the leaders of the Union Council. The precise contents did not become clear until after the Union Council had instituted certain measures.

We have already seen that many believing Evangelical Christians/Baptists did not much appreciate state-imposed regulations. When, therefore, the Union Council in 1961 issued new statutes and sent to the senior presbyters a letter in which it conformed to the secret demands of the government, serious opposition arose. Both the content of the instructions and statutes and also the manner in which they were presented provided the blow that led to the formation of an organized opposition group. In 1966 in the magazine *Nauka i Religia*,[90] an article appeared on the origin of this group. Named after one of its most prominent leaders, A. F. Prokofiev, it was called the Prokofiev Group. In comparison with other Soviet publications on Prokofiev, this article is quite objective in character.

> The official date of the emergence of the Prokofiev Group was, according to them, August 13, 1961, which marked the beginning of the "internal church movement demanding a congress, a renewal, and a re-dedication of our Evangelical Baptist brotherhood." On that day the so-called Action Group released its first appeal signed by Prokofiev and Kryuchkov.
>
> From 1960, with the general decrease in the number of believers, the conflict of groups of people who had not joined the Evangelical Christians and Baptists became fiercer.
>
> In these conditions A. Prokofiev cunningly exploited the fact that the all-Union Council had responded to the wish of the majority of believers

actively to participate in the building of Communism.

Most believers were urging the lifting of the ban on visiting theatres and cinemas; they wanted to listen to the radio and to watch television and to renounce forcible religious upbringing for their children and young people.

Those who have gone into schism produce several underground publications.

What is the content of this literature?

Prokofiev's followers assign first place to religious legal problems, both internal church ones and those which relate exclusively to the authority of the state. They write a good deal about self-sacrifice in the name of Christ and the necessity of suffering for the faith. Those who suffer in Christ's name are extolled as people "who have received baptism in the name of the Holy Spirit." In one of his recent works A. Prokofiev made three demands upon believers: separation, sanctification, and dedication in the specific sense of self-sacrifice in the name of Christ.

A more precise exegesis of this little article is necessary in order to arrive at an accurate picture of what actually took place. Six points stand out here.

1. There is a group within the brotherhood of Evangelical Christians/Baptists that wants to hold a congress and to push for internal renewal. It is called the Action Group—in Russian, *Initsiativnaya gruppa*, from whence comes their name Initsiativniki.

2. The group prints a number of illegal publications. The most important ones are *Bratskii Listok* (Brotherhood Magazine) and *Vestnik Spasenia* (The Salvation Herald).

Michael Bourdeaux, who in his book *Religious Ferment in Russia*: *Protestant Opposition to Soviet Religious Policy* gives the most extensive documentation on the Initsiativniki, has published detailed material from these little magazines.

3. Mention is made of the decrease in the number of believers and at the same time of the existence of groups of believers not affiliated with the Evangelical Christians/Baptists. We have already written about the compulsory registration of congregations as well as about the difficulties often experienced at registration. Different groups were thereby forced into an illegal existence and delivered up to the arbitrariness of the authorities, with whom difficulties could erupt at any moment. The decrease in membership is related to the measures taken by the government that led to the dissolving and combining of congregations.

For example—also from the Soviet press—there is the known case of the Evangelical Christian/Baptist congregation in Brest which, in 1960, was combined with the congregation in the little village of Vulla in the Brest district. Of the 380 members, only 100 went to Vulla; the rest organized "illegal" meetings in private homes in the city. Thus there arose opposition on the part of the church membership against the church leadership which had allowed this to happen. The story is repeated again and again. In 1962 the congregation in Leningrad was compelled to close the church in the center of the city and move to an out-of-the-way suburb. They received the use of a small Orthodox church in Troickoye Polye. The "decline in the number of believers" is mostly due to the fact that groups have come to stand outside the bond of the Union of Evangelical Christians/Baptists. Their number is estimated at from five to eight per cent.

4. The Union Council of the Evangelical Christians/Baptists supposedly submitted to the desire of the majority

of the believers to take an active part in the progress of Communism and to give up coercive religious education of the children and young people. It is striking enough that an atheistic paper here writes positively about the Union Council of Evangelical Christians/Baptists. What precisely is meant by the "desire to take an active part in the progress of Communism" is not immediately clear. At any rate, it is a positive judgment of a step which the leadership of the Evangelical Christians/Baptists had taken and which the opposition opposed. How far that is related to the religious training of the children remains to be seen. In the underground press of the Initsiativniki, constant reference is made to this.

5. The followers of Prokofiev strongly emphasize the problems concerning the relation between church and state. We shall return to that in a separate chapter.

6. They write a great deal about self-sacrifice and how necessary it is not to shun suffering for the faith. The large number of captured and sentenced Initsiativniki—a list of more than 200 names is included in the aforementioned book of Bourdeaux, and a list of 176 names of captured believers is to be found in *Dein Reich komme* of January and December, 1970, and September and November, 1971 — certainly makes clear that in any case the information of the atheist writer is correct here.

We shall now enter more fully into a discussion of the action of the Initsiativniki, using especially their own publications as Bourdeaux reproduces them.

XI. The Congress

At the same time that new statutes were issued at the beginning of the new period of church persecution in 1960, the Union Council of the Evangelical Christians/Baptists sent out a letter with instructions to the senior presbyters. Of this letter, the following was written in *Bratskii Listok* (February-March, 1965):[91]

> In your new statutes and particularly in your letter of instructions you disobeyed the commandment of Christ by prescribing the following:
>
> Par. 4: At services a presbyter must not allow digressions which tend to become appeals...
>
> Par. 5: Zealous proselytization in our communities must definitely stop... and an effort must be made to reduce the baptisms of young people between 18 and 30 years to a minimum.
>
> Disobeying the commandment of Christ ("Suffer little children and forbid them not to come unto me"—Matt. 19: 14), you prescribed that:
>
> Par. 6: Children... should not be allowed to attend services. You have issued many other similar instructions. With these "documents" and "statutes" you have denied salvation to the sinner; when salvation is denied, then it follows there is no need for a Saviour. Through

this, then, you have rejected even the Saviour Himself. And all this has been done to pander to atheism and to the world.

After the new statutes became known, Prokofiev and Kryuchkov took the initiative to convene a special congress at which the drafting of new statutes would be discussed. They sent a letter to all registered and non-registered congregations, an action which revealed grave suspicions about the leadership of the Union in Moscow. The Union was reproached for allowing itself to be tied to the apron strings of the state, for not being chosen by the delegates of the local churches, not respecting the rights of the local churches, hindering the mission task as the most important commission of the church, and retarding the proclamation of the Gospel to children and young people.

Thus it appeared from the letter that there existed a deep chasm between the leadership and a part of the believers, and a grave suspicion regarding the Council leaders. The Initsiativniki also drafted new statutes intended to give the congregations a voice in the leading and life of the Union in a much clearer way. This would also eliminate the possibility of the state exercising control over the internal life of the Union and the congregations by its intervening in the leadership. As presented by the Initsiativniki, the statutes would establish clearly that the governing body, the Union Council, must be elected by a congress of delegates and thereby would hold a less unassailable position than it had held in fact up to that time. There had to be more local autonomy and less control from the top. The position of the senior presbyters had to change. They must be elected by regional conferences of delegates from the district and not appointed by the Union Council. In themselves, these wishes by the Initsiativniki are very reasonable and in harmony with the democratic traditions of both the Evangelical Christians and of the Baptists.

The leadership in Moscow, however, did not initially discuss these proposals. Probably it could do little else, for the pressure from the authorities upon them at that moment was heavier and more serious than the pressure they felt from the Union. Yet it soon became clear that the problem here concerned a serious opposition group with a large following, especially in the Ukrainian congregations. Already by the end of November, 1961, the Union Council discussed with a number of senior presbyters what measures would have to be taken. It was understood that this group, which wanted to call things clearly and openly by their name and in airing their grievances would not spare the authorities, might pose a real danger to the Union's position in the country. In *Bratskii Vestnik* (November 6, 1963)[92] this concern was clearly articulated :

> We warn all our brothers and sisters against various sorts of persons who endanger the whole work of the Lord in our country, because they represent an attempt to bring our brotherhood into sharper conflict with the authorities and the leaders of our country. This threatens not only our entire brotherhood but also runs counter to the whole spirit of the Gospel and the teaching of our Lord Jesus Christ.

The negative attitude of the Union Council, which at first formally wanted to overlook the Initsiativniki, strengthened the latter in their suspicions that the Union Council was indeed tied to the apron strings of the state and solidified the opposition all the more. In a resolution of March 22, 1962, the Initsiativniki formulated the following accusations against the Union Council : [93]

1. Of putting into effect anti-evangelical docu-

ments (the new statutes and the letter of instructions) not confirmed by the church.

2. Of including in the Union only a third of the communities (registered), while two-thirds (unregistered) have not been recognized by it.

3. Of conducting hostile activities against the convocation of an all-union congress, in opposition to the demands of the whole church.

4. In the light of the above statements and also guided by God's Word, particularly Hebrews 12: 15, I Corinthians 5: 12-13, Galatians 5: 10, 12, and the words of Christ, we declare: "And if he neglect to hear the Church, let him be to you as a heathen man and a publican" (Matt. 18: 17b).

The violent intervention by the authorities and the persecution of the Initsiativniki that began soon after their action was publicized were particularly lamentable. It has intensified the contrasts and strengthened the power and depth of the opposition. In most cases they were persecuted on the basis of the so-called "parasite regulation" of May 4, 1961, which "was concerned with the strengthening of the fight against people who avoid socially useful work and who lead an antisocial parasitic form of life."[94] On the basis of this vague and elastic article the authorities could sentence the Initsiativniki, who unwearyingly traveled to all corners of the country visiting their partisans, to prison terms of two to five years. Prokofiev in 1962 was sentenced to five years in prison and many others suffered the same fate. Four leaders of the congregation in Brest entered prison for three or five years. Another got three years because he led an illegal Baptist sect and made converts in Alma-Ata. His worst offense was that he allowed his son to join the congregation.

One of the most moving documents of the trials against the Initsiativniki is the report of the Odessa trial

141

that took place from February 2 to 7, 1967. A report of the trial appeared in German translation in *Light in the East*. Five men and two women, members of the church in Peresip, a suburb of Odessa, received a sentence of three years. Their church was confiscated in 1958. A number of church members, however, continued to hold meetings in homes and sometimes in a wood. Though time and again they had requested registration from the authorities, it was refused. They were thus persecuted on the ground of overstepping the laws regarding the exercise of religion. Present at the trial were fellow members who made a report of the court session. This report and especially the defense speeches of the accused give a moving description of convinced Christians devoted entirely to the right, that they might confess their faith in freedom. Christians who dared to give a courageous testimony before the judge. One of them concluded with the words:

> Whatever way I must go, I shall remain true to the Lord. But to you, citizen judge, I must say that no czar and no judge has remained unpunished for conducting an unrighteous trial. I want you to think about that. Now is the accepted time, now is the day of salvation; tomorrow, life is not in your hand.

One of the most remarkable reactions to these arrests and convictions was the formation of a committee of the relatives of Evangelical Christian/Baptist prisoners. The object of this was to give publicity to the fate of prisoners and to the children who had been taken away from their parents because they were receiving a religious upbringing. Both through this committee and the illegal publications of the Initsiativniki, more came to be known about these events. The action taken by the government has made the solution to the conflict particularly difficult, and the contrast between the persecuted and the tolerated Evangelical Christians/Baptists was naturally heightened. The leadership in Moscow came to stand in a most unsavory position. Of course they did not at all welcome this sort of intervention, but how easily could the violence of the authorities be laid at their door! Moreover, a dialogue with the opposition had now become practically impossible. The state convicted people because they stood outside the bond of the Union of Evangelical Christians/ Baptists. The state tried to silence an opposition group which was alarmed about the religious establishment and drive them back with the whip into the ghetto wherein the church might live. But the Initsiativniki were not so easy to manipulate.

In August, 1963, they wrote a letter to Khrushchev urging that a special congress be held at which the two groups might discuss with each other the regulation of the life of the church. There was no reaction to that letter. In October, 1963, however, the Union Council did convene a congress of church delegates in Moscow, the first after the war. Without lessening the pressure on the Initsiativniki, the authorities evidently thought to take the wind out of the sails of the opposition by giving permission for the congress to convene. The letter of instruction was recalled and a new constitution was adopted in which many of the points to which the Initsiativniki objected were met in a spirit of compromise. In particular it was established that every three years a general meeting of delegates from the churches was to be held (in 1969 because of organizational reasons this was changed to four or five years); that the Union Council was to be chosen by this general meeting; that the congregations were to have greater independence in regard to the senior presbyter. Important changes, and the Initsiativniki might have been satisfied. But they themselves were absent from the congress because the majority of their leaders were in prison and probably also because the chasm between the two groups had grown too wide. The Initsiativniki had excommunicated the leaders of the church, among them Y. Zhidkov, A. V. Karev, and I. G. Ivanov, and banned them from the fellowship of faith. In September, 1965, they constituted themselves as a council of churches of the Evangelical Christians/Baptists and thus clearly showed they were traveling the road leading to a complete break and the building of their own church union. Even though immediately after this congress the Union Council had good hope that unity could be restored, reconciliation never materialized. It had done its best for it, and as the changes in the new statutes showed, it had made a solid contribution. Naturally, we must be aware of the fact that the congress could not have accepted these changes if the leaders had not been able to win the authorities' support for them earlier. Moreover, the Union Council promised to help all it could with the registering of congregations, with the acquisition and maintenance of church buildings, and with the defending of the rights and interests of individual congregations and presbyters.

But the chasm was altogether too deep, and the concern was no longer merely to change the statutes. It was no longer a matter of church order; other points of difference, difficult for an outsider to understand, played a background role. More profound theological differences seem to have been involved in the conflict. We have already spoken of the schismatic movement in the middle of the 50's when many who returned from prison camps opposed co-operation between Evangelical Christians, Baptists, and Pentecostal groups within the Union. In the 60's there were no doubt "pure" Baptists involved in the schism of the Initsiativniki. Other motives, inspired by old differences between Evangelical Christians and Baptists, also entered the picture, for example, the greater openness of Evangelical Christians to culture. I. S. Prochanov pleaded in the 20's not only for a strong evangelism movement but also for an active participation in the development of science and art. Among the Baptists, however, one finds more of a "thumbs-down" attitude toward culture. The Old Testament tenor in the publications by the Initsiativniki; their emphasis on the expectation of the return of Christ and the necessity for the sanctification and purification of the church; their accusation that, as in Pergamum (Rev. 2: 13), Satan has erected his throne in the church, that a Laodicean Christianity has stolen into the church (Rev. 3: 15), that a sort of culture-Christianity has arisen, that by joining the World Council of Churches a new kind of Babylon has arisen—all these things indicate that their action was taken not merely because of a question of church order, but because of a vision of the Christian faith and life which does not so much deviate from the others as insist on a more radical stance. A group discovers that the power of faith is diminishing and that people are becoming careless, that they seek to compromise with the world too easily, that they are taken in by modern living with its many possibilities but also its many temptations. They ask whether the church belongs to Christ the Lord who alone is its Head or to the state and thus the world. And they summon their fellow believers to greater Christian responsibility, to more intensive involvement in the life of the church, to a more active evangelism, to a fiercer resistance against the dangerous infiltration of the government's influence.

These phenomena recur in the life of each church and are well known from history. But the situation in Russia is infinitely more complicated than in other countries, where the church has the opportunity to solve its own problems independently. In the Soviet Union the complicating factor is intervention by the state. The state is not only atheistically focused in theory but is actively bent on eliminating the Christian church. As long as the church exists, however, the state wants to dam up its influence as much as possible, while at the same time using it as much as possible for its own purposes. In actual practice there is no separation of church and state as guaranteed in the Soviet constitution. The leadership of the church is bound by this situation and has only limited opportunity to deal with the partially justifiable reproaches and complaints. The congresses of 1963 and 1966, at which the church statutes were changed even more in the direction of the Initsiativniki, are proof of the desire to react positively to the complaints. The election of senior presbyters was now also put into practice, and congregations were given greater independence. The Union Council was enlarged to twenty-five members. From this augmented Union Council a presidium consisting of ten members was chosen, the majority of which were old members. The fierceness and the strong personal bias of the Initsiativniki grievances are factors which perhaps should have been apprehended with greater wisdom. The open letter of December, 1967, undersigned by Secretary-general Alexander V. Karev and President I. G. Ivanov, was sent to the churches abroad with the intent of squelching[95] rumors about a split within the Union. It is a somewhat less sympathetic document that had better not been written. The following passage is quite ambiguous :

> People in our country are not persecuted on account of their religious conviction; rather, to our deep regret, a few of our brothers and sisters were called to account because they had not obeyed the laws regarding religion and because they had disturbed the public order.

The sending of this letter was evidently inspired by the desire to neutralize the influence of the protest letter which some months before had been sent to the secretary-general of the United Nations by relatives of the Baptist prisoners. In that letter of August 15, 1967, it was stated:

> We would not have turned to an international

organization if there had been the slightest hope that our requests to the government of the U.S.S.R. would have brought about positive results. But the cruel war against the non-registered congregations is being broadened ... We ask you, Mr. U Thant, to do everything possible that is considered safe, regarding :

1. the freedom of religion
2. the right of parents to bring up their children to maturity.[96]

To what extent the Union Council letter was written at the direction of a higher hand is impossible to ascertain. Official statements by Russian church delegates regarding freedom of religion must always be taken with a grain of salt. Commentary from *Light in the East*: how far this ecclesiastical diplomacy brought the leaders of the Union Council to a secret "martyrdom of lies," we can only surmise.[97] We know[98] from a report of the 1966 congress that a telegram was sent to the authorities with the request that the sentences of the captured Initsiativniki leaders be softened. "When the intercessory prayer for the imprisoned brethren was offered, the tears of the official leaders mingled with those of the brethren who belonged to the secession." However, this brotherly attitude of compassion for the persecuted described in the report is missing in the letter. The Union leaders did, however, admit that sending the letter of instruction and formulating new statutes in 1960 had been a serious error, an admission which was repeated very clearly in 1969.

Simultaneously with the intensive attempts by the Evangelical Christians/Baptists to heal the schism and to restore unity by visiting congregations and by holding conversations with diverse groups and currents within the Union, government pressure increased once more. In March, 1966, new regulations, with special reference to the Initsiativniki, were issued in which the failure to register organizations started by religious leaders, the performance of fraudulent tricks designed to foster superstition among the populace, the organizing of student and young peoples' meetings by members of religious societies, even when they served literary or other purposes, were all made punishable with a fine of fifty rubles, and if repeated, a prison sentence of three years.[99] It seems it is precisely the religious education and upbringing of the youth which is under fire by the state. Repeatedly in the reports of the persecutions, mention is made of children removed from under the authority of the parents and reared in state institutions. The action taken against the religious influencing of under-age children is not an isolated phenomenon, the work of a few party fanatics. It is the official political line about which it was said in 1963, in a speech to the Ideological Committee at a party congress :

> We cannot and must not remain indifferent to the fate of the children on whom parents, fanatical believers, are inflicting spiritual violence. We cannot allow blind and ignorant parents to rear their children to become like themselves and so to deform them.[100]

The Central Committee of the party decided, therefore, to extend the supervision designed to protect children and young people from churchly influences. Moreover, parents are not permitted to demand from their children the observance of religious customs.

The fact that children are removed by the state from the influence of their parents appears in many reports. In a paper of the Young Communist League[101] a photograph was published of four kneeling children with the following caption :

> These children have done no harm. It was their Pentecostal parents who obliged them to kneel. We can say at once that this photograph is out

of date. The four children seen here have been removed from the guardianship of fanatical believers. But they are not the last victims of religious despotism. Our duty as Komsomols and elder brothers is to guard every child from the attacks of religious fanaticism.

In November, 1966, the following was reported in a White Russian newspaper : [102]

> The facts show that in the re-training of believers not all forms of individual action are being used. This can explain why Anna Nepolsk remains in ranks of the Baptists even to this day. Fortunately, it was possible to rescue Anna's children from this. They have been placed in the Disenk boarding school. But how many like Anna are still left in the area ?

It is certainly clear that these stories of children being taken from parental influence are not fables of anti-Soviet propagandists, but hard, cruel facts.

Attempts are made in other ways to obstruct the Christian life. New administrative measures, for example, were taken to prevent the baptism of children. This measure, naturally, struck only at the Orthodox believers and not at the Evangelical Christians and Baptists, who do not believe in infant baptism. It illustrates the attitude of the authorities, which requires that at baptism a certificate be produced which states that the godfather lives and works locally. In this way the authorities know who has his child baptized and they can exert pressure on the parents, particularly upon the father. The fact that it is made more difficult for young people to attend church services has already been mentioned.

In the years 1966 and 1967 the Soviet press systematically harassed the Evangelical Christians and Baptists, making repeated disclosures of the believers' pernicious influence upon the youth. A teacher discovered a group in one home: [103]

> The children sat around a table and were learning prayers and psalms; a Bible was lying open on the table, and for each child there was a notebook in which they copied "texts."

The story of one case of government action against what we call the Sunday School may now be fully told. Moreover, we get an idea of the believers' activities. [104] On March 11, Maria Braun (born in 1946, living in the village of Archangelsk in the Kirghiz S.S.R.) and a friend were sentenced to five years in a work camp. From the court notes, the following :

> Maria Braun and her friend belong to a non-registered congregation of the Evangelical Christians and Baptists. Since the year 1964 they organized and led a religious school for children in Novopavlovka. Through her initiative and active participation more than eighty pre-school children were taught in this school. The local authorities warned the accused repeatedly about their illegal behavior of teaching children in a religious school. Yet the two accused continued to lead the religious school and to set up a curriculum and thereby poison the nature of the children by keeping them isolated from society. In their teaching they make use of an ideology alien to the Soviet system and urge the children to refuse to join Soviet youth organizations. A fifth-grade student from the elementary school, who attended the religious instruction of the accused, wrote the following to the council of the Young Pioneers on October 14, 1965 : "I request that you exclude me from the Young Pioneers because on account of my faith I can-

not wear the red kerchief . . ." Both the accused pleaded innocent and refused to give any further explanations.

In the letter to U Thant in 1967 it was said :

> Maria Braun, who is staying in a camp in the province of Perm, was denied the right to accept food packages for one year. According to the administration, that is an educational measure.

In a report on the twenty-three-year-old Maria Braun, dated May, 1970, we are told that she was taken to a more severe detention camp. To the deep sorrow of her parents she lost her faith and no longer prays. To every active atheist opponent of religion, this report must give a great deal of satisfaction.

From December 9 to 11, 1969, a Union congress was again held, at which some 478 delegates from every Soviet republic took part.[105] The leaders of the Initsiativniki were invited but refused to be present as mere guests. The relationship toward the separate council of the Initsiativniki churches was naturally once more on the agenda. Mention was made of four meetings between representatives of the Union Council and the Initsiativniki, Vins, and Kryuchkov. At the last meeting held on December 4, 1969, they declared their acceptance of the expressed act of penitence made in 1966 by the leaders of the Union Council for errors committed. No concrete steps, however, were taken toward a reunion. From this it appears that the separation did indeed stem from a deeper, more fundamental character than merely from a formal question of church order. The process of mutual estrangement that has taken place in these ten years is not easily turned and healed. It seems, however, that the government has been making a few more concessions to the Union Council in the last few years, perhaps to strengthen somewhat the position of the governing body within the Union of Evangelical Christians and Baptists. Permission to print Bibles and hymnals, the organization of a course for ministers, and opportunity for theologians to study in England point in this direction.

The Initsiativniki were also given permission to hold a conference. This took place on December 6, 1969, in Tula, where 120 delegates had come together. Leading figures in the Separate Council of Churches considered the permission to hold this congress a first step toward the recognition of their council as an independent federation alongside of the Union of 1944. All congregations were advised to request recognition and registration from the local government, and exemption for the minister from any obligation to occupy a secular trade.[106]

After reading these reports the impression might arise that the pressure is somewhat eased. It is very difficult to evaluate the situation. On March 16, 1970, the Council of Family Relatives of prisoners from the churches of Evangelical Christians/Baptists directed an urgent appeal to the Soviet government, since it had done nothing about illegal persecution despite information it had received about it. There is mention made of nine new arrests, among them three brothers who had played a leading role at the officially permitted conference in Tula. It seems especially difficult for the Initsiativniki to achieve legality, since in the present state of affairs they would really be forced to deny their own principles. After all, their protest does not merely concern itself with the democratizing of the church organization and greater independence for the local congregations, questions upon which the official Union judged them to be in the right. Their protest is directed especially against state intervention in the internal life of the church, the constant attempts to shrink the spiritual living space of the church and to synchronize ideological differences, and above all, against the regulations concerning religious upbringing. It looks like this opposition, not against the official union

152

leadership but against specific aspects of the Soviet regime, is not about to end for the present. They have involved themselves in an extreme fundamental conflict with the Soviet authorities for the broadening of their civic rights, and they carry on the battle for another relationship between church and state with courage and conviction. Their conflict, it is true, does not receive the attention in the Netherlands that writers and intellectuals receive, but it is an older phenomenon and is also clearly rooted in another stratum of the population. In the famous television conversation of August, 1970, in which four Russian authors articulated their protest against the regime and pleaded for more civic and democratic liberties, Amalrik said, among other things :

> I have had many contacts with factory workers and farmers, and I get the impression that they have not yet really begun to reflect on the nature of this system; as far as their feeling is concerned, it has always been this way and will always remain so.

He is obviously not informed about the activities of the separated Evangelical Christians/Baptists, who have their illegal periodicals such as the literary *Samizdat* and have made their protests clearly audible, on account of which many hundreds are in prisons and camps. We have already mentioned the Odessa trial. In March, 1969, another trial was held for nine Evangelical Christians/Baptists. In response, a letter was sent to the government and party leaders by 180 believing young people, in which they protested the unduly severe sentences, requested religious freedom and freedom to witness, and asked that the way to learning might be opened for young people who wanted to be Christian. Discrimination against believers who want to enroll in institutions of learning and build a career is evident but difficult to accept. It is understandable that someone once lamented that in the

Soviet Union one is the slave of the freest constitution. In November, 1969, a letter[107] addressed "to all Christian churches and to all Christians in the world" was published by the Council of Family Relatives of imprisoned members of the Evangelical Christians/Baptists, a letter from 1,453 mothers in forty-two Russian cities. Mention is made of their relatives' martyrdom, the closing of churches, the deportation of children, and the confiscation of writings. Attached to this letter is a list of the names of 176 prisoners and the places of their confinement, together with the number of dependent members in each family. This concerns believers arrested and convicted after 1966. The action by the Initsiativniki has great political significance. Admiration for "the increasing recklessness"[108] of the resistance of writers and intellectuals must not make us forget the courage, steadfastness, and spiritual power with which these simple believers fight for more spiritual freedom, a purifying of the relationship of church and state, and a change in the constitution.

XII. Separation of Church and State

The Initsiativniki, who at first emerged as an opposition group within the Union of Evangelical Christians/Baptists, developed more and more into an open protest movement against the continual interventions by the Soviet government in the religious life of the citizens and in the internal life of the church. One could also say that they discovered their real adversaries with ever greater clarity. These are not to be found in the leadership of their churches but in the leadership of their state. The Initsiativniki did not intend to fight the socialist system as such, nor the Soviet authorities as such. In 1961 they even sent a flattering message to the Communist Party Congress, which stated : [109]

> Having read the draft of the Communist Party program for building Communism in our country we Christians are also happy that many of us who write these lines will be able to live under Communism; and we, together with all Soviet citizens, are contributing our work and our knowledge so that in our country we may more rapidly achieve an abundance of food products, consumer goods, equipment, and automatic

devices and a growth of moral qualities and culture. What a wonderful sound have the sublime words of the Party Program: "Man is a friend, comrade, and brother to his fellow-man."

This message may seem altogether too submissive and docile, yet it contains a clear position. From it we see that the Initsiativniki clearly accept the socio-economic order of the Communist regime, and the position that this order can promote brotherhood and humanity; it does not, however, say that they accept the Communist ideology as a world-and-life view. They proceed from the premise that a separation, or at least a distinction, can be made between dialectical materialism as a world-and-life view and historic materialism as a socio-economic principle. They have as the starting-point of their view the conception of a state which is ideologically neutral, and they resist both a one-sided interpretation of the constitution and the monopolistic attitude of a party which, according to their insights, runs counter to the constitution. They plead for an actual observance of Article 124 of the constitution, in which freedom of conscience and the separation of church and state and church and school is anchored. In actual practice the constitutional article of the separation of church and state has proved to be a fiction.[110] Kolarz calls it a hypocritical article of the law.[111] It suggests a separation and an independence of church and state which in fact does not exist, and which the state does not wish to exist. Actually this article should guarantee the freedom of the church and the neutrality of the state in everything that concerns religion. But this is not the case. The Soviet Union does not function as that article suggests and as representatives of "loyal" religious organizations constantly affirm : as "an ideologically neutral, impartial constitutional state, which gives equal protection to believers and unbelievers."[112] It is a "con-

156

fessional" state, wherein the ideology of the Communist Party has taken the place of the former, monopolistic, czarist state church with self-evident logic. In my view there are two fundamental problems relative to religious freedom and the separation of church and state in Russia. There is, first of all, this historical relationship between church and state. There the process of secularization, which had already run its course in Western Europe, had, prior to 1917, barely begun. No tradition of religious freedom did emerge that one could draw on for precedent. A remarkable dialogue took place at the hearing of one of the accused in the Odessa trial in 1967.

> The judge asks: "You have preached and you do not consider that a transgression?" The accused: "In the sense that you mean it, I have not preached. But all believers are preachers of God's Kingdom." Judge: "Imagine the following scene: everyone begins to preach in our country, whatever he desires and wherever he chooses, regardless of whether he is listened to or not." Accused: "I would speak only about Christ and only where people would listen and had asked me to do so."

This dialogue is remarkable because of the observation of the judge, who probably in perfect honesty cannot imagine what this world is coming to if each one has the liberty to preach or not to preach. Where might he have gained the experience that it was then still possible to live together? A pluralistic society in which a free confrontation of different spiritual and world-view conceptions is possible is something Russia has never known. Certain groups of Evangelical Christians/Baptists are now pleading for that with all their might. Their starting point is that it must be possible for a free church to exist in the Soviet Union, and they resist the "Communist orthodoxy" that wants to control the spiritual life of all citizens as once they resisted the "czarist orthodoxy" that could tolerate dissenters only insofar that they were and remained foreigners.

The second problem in connection with religious freedom is that fundamental and militant atheism has acquired a monopolistic position and that the totalitarian structure of society has been placed in the service of atheism. Yet the separation of church and state is being defended by different Communist parties in the West. In 1967 the Italian Communist party turned away from all "automatic atheism" and rejected the idea that the state should give "an ideology, philosophy, or religion, or a cultural or artistic school, special privileges detrimental to others."[113] Theoretically such a separation should be possible, since Marxism teaches that the illusion of religion will vanish of itself when a healthy social arrangement has been established. According to that principle it should not be necessary to fight religion actively. After all, it will die itself. But probably the situation of the Communist Party in the Soviet Union, which controls the state, is different from that of the parties in Italy or France. As is evident from the measures taken against the turbulent intellectuals, it fights back vigorously against every attempt to secularize the system, that is to say, to bring about separation of state power and ideology. It does not want to give up its directing and controlling grip on all aspects of life, on all social relations and even on the private lives of citizens. The church groups that exist in Russia are, by the very fact that they exist, a sign of protest against a uniform totalitarian society. We see, however, in the 60's the rise within the churches of a movement which does not only wish to give a quiet testimony of perseverance and patience, but which actively wants to fight for greater spiritual freedom. In doing so, it gives itself a sort of constitutional status by clearly making an appeal to the constitution and the separation of church and state anchored therein. We can no longer call these groups an "underground" or a "catacomb" church, for one of their striking features is precisely the fact that they carry out their activities in broad daylight, that they address themselves to their own government and to world opinion. They consider meddling of the state in church affairs and the atheistic indoctrination in the schools to be in conflict with the constitution.

On April 14, 1965, the Initsiativniki addressed themselves in a letter to the highest Soviet authorities, in particular to Brezhnev as president of a state committee to review the constitution. The letter is written by Gennadi Kryuchkov and Georgi Vins, two leading figures in the Initsiativniki. It is a moving document and gives a clear survey of the development of the relation of the state to the churches, or to put it more precisely, of the restriction of religious freedom—the curtailment of the freedom to confess one's faith and to testify to it resulting in a limited freedom to hold religious services. The restriction is that religious fellowships must be registered by the state, yet this registration is often made impossible through the arbitrariness of administrative apparatus. It requires registration but refuses to register, and thus possesses itself of an argument to prohibit illegal meetings and to take measures against participants.

Against this interpretation of the constitution and the measures taken that are grounded in it, the action and resistance of the Initsiativniki is aimed. They have not only made their protest heard by the sending of letters, but also by demonstrations and the presentation of petitions and objections to local and regional authorities. Thus on May 16, 1966, five hundred believers from all parts of the country came to Moscow and held a demonstration at the building of the Central Committee of the Communist Party. They submitted a written petition in which they asked that persecutions might stop and that separated

159

groups might be recognized. They remained there a day and a half until they were finally removed.

It is necessary here to point to the protest also of the Orthodox Church directed against the same subject, namely, the arbitrary, unofficial, and unlawful control brought to bear on the churches by the state, which constitutes an attack upon the legislation regarding the separation of church and state and school and church. At the end of 1965 open letters to the bishops of the Russian Orthodox Church appeared, written by the Moscow priests Nikolai Eshliman and Khlev Yakunin. We shall not reproduce these letters here[114] but do want to point to the strong parallels. These letters too are an accusation against the subjective and arbitrary application and interpretation of Soviet legislation, and they upbraid the church leaders for completely submitting to the secret oral instructions of the authorities. Their action and their reproofs are analogous to those of the Initsiativniki and can also be seen as an important contribution to the striving after greater spiritual freedom and a more pluralistic society in the Soviet Union. A few aspects of the relationship of the Orthodox Church to the state and of the problem of the so-called underground church are treated in an article appearing at the end of this book.

It is a sign of intense spiritual life in the churches that the problems created by the relationship of church and state and church and society are repeatedly formulated so clearly in the most recent history of the Soviet churches. One no longer submits to the enslavement of the church and the restriction of spiritual life. It is also beginning to look as if the regime is finding it increasingly difficult to silence these voices. If we bear in mind that the Initsiativniki involve only a relatively small number of people, one is amazed that so powerful a country as the Soviet Union deals as fiercely with them as it does. Probably behind this phenomenon is the realization that it concerns a very real and fundamental matter. The question may also be posed whether the regime still has enough inner power to survive a genuine confrontation with this group.

For it has certainly proved true that the Initsiativniki joined the conflict for freedom of the church completely and with great willingness to sacrifice. And they no longer stand alone. The protest actions of writers and intellectuals who also struggle for greater spiritual and cultural freedom are in the line of the actions of the Initsiativniki.

When one studies the various documents bearing on the Initsiativniki one must come to the conclusion that they will not be eliminated easily. The outcome of the conflict is difficult to predict. At the present it looks as if they will be squeezed to death by the powerful state apparatus which has all the means of power at its disposal. But, as G. C. Borushko said in his defense at the aforementioned Odessa trial :

> I am an optimist, that is to say, I believe that if things go badly now, tomorrow they will go better. If one is condemned now, tomorrow one will be acquitted. If on earth one must now suffer injustice, tomorrow justice will appear. Such is the dialectic. If the church doesn't find confirmation on earth, yet in heaven she shall triumph, even as it is written: "According to his promise, we look for new heavens and a new earth, wherein dwelleth righteousness."

Appendix:

Between Loyalty and Martyrdom

Is there an underground church in Russia ?

At the national synod of the Russian Orthodox Church which met for the first time since 1945 in the Trinity St. Sergius Monastery in Zagorsk from May 3 to June 2, 1971, the sixty-year-old metropolitan Pimen was elected the new patriarch of Moscow and all Russia. This event received scant notice in the Dutch press and in church periodicals, as did the death of the ninety-two-year-old patriarch Alexi in April, 1970, after a patriarchate of twenty-five years.

Our interest in the Orthodox Church in Russia is clearly less now than some ten years ago. After the Russian churches joined the World Council of Churches in New Delhi in 1961, there was a renewed interest in the life of the church in an atheist, Communist country and some sympathy for the hierarchs of that church when they appeared in the West at ecclesiastical meetings. At present, however, a critical and often somewhat negative tone is dominant in certain circles. Along with this there is a certain critical attitude toward the World Council of Churches. There are those who think it takes too little action against the persecutions. Behind this observation one hears something of a reproach that contacts are maintained with the official church representatives from Eastern Europe, from whom protests against persecution might be expected but from whom one hears nothing. Among those who are opposed to or hesitant about the World Council, a fairly strong influence is that of the Rumanian evangelist Richard Wurmbrand, supported by the I.C.C.C. (International Council of Christian Churches), operating out of America. He is strongly anti-communist and fiercely attacks everyone who keeps up ecumenical contacts with Eastern Europe. We shall speak more directly about his activity below.

Recently, a certain change in popular thinking has taken place. We shall examine the reasons for this, subsuming them in three points :

1. *Criticism of the leadership of the church*

In the last few years there has been an increasing number of reports of new persecutions against churches and individual believers during Khrushchev's regime. From 1959 to 1964 the state waged a fierce anti-religious campaign which had first and foremost an administrative character.

One can distinguish different phases in the conflict of the Communist government with the church. From 1918 to 1929 the conflict was aimed especially at destroying the position of the privileged State Church. From 1929 to 1940 an attempt was made to eliminate all religious life and all religious activity. One can state that, insofar as it concerned institutional church life, this effort quite succeeded, particularly in the years 1937 and 1938. The clergy was deported, the churches (with an occasional exception) were locked up, and when the war broke out, there were only four bishops active. The war brought about a change in this apparently hopeless situation and a new period of growth became possible. Metropolitan Sergii was elected patriarch in 1943 and an orderly church life once more developed, especially after the death of Stalin in 1953. But in 1959 there came an end to this period of thaw. A number of new measures were taken to limit the growing influence of the church in the life of the people and to strengthen the grip of the state in the affairs of the church.

In 1965 two Moscow priests, N. Eshliman and K. Yakunin, wrote an open letter to Patriarch Alexi in which they reproached the patriarch for having surrendered too much to the pressure of the state, and then recounted a number of measures and incidents: the large-scale shutting of churches and monasteries, especially in the new areas added to the U.S.S.R. after the war, which was often accompanied by serious violence to the monks, as was the case in the shutting of the Pokayev monastery not far from Lvov (now open once more); registration of baptisms and other church ceremonies, so that the participants subsequently can be placed under administrative pressure at work and school; prohibiting services in private homes and in cemeteries; the prevention of children taking part in the life of the church; the influence of the state in the appointment of clergy; and other regulations regarding the taxes of the clergy and limiting their sphere of labor.

The two priests reproved the prominent bishops for being too willing to serve as tools in carrying out regulations and measures aimed against the welfare of the church and for keeping themselves too quiet out of fear for the position of the church. Their letter was supported by eight bishops under the leadership of archbishop Yermogen of Kaluga, who because of his role was forced to step down and retire to a monastery, despite his being one of the most prominent Russian church leaders. The two priests were deposed from office, but as far as we know, no further measures were taken against them.

A. E. Levitin (who also published under the name Krasnov), born in 1915, minister and writer of articles for, among others, the *Journal of the Moscow Patriarchate*, prisoner from 1949 to 1956 and one of the best-known figures among the church opposition, wrote an article on the patriarch and his staff in which this sentence occurs: [115] "In the days when churches were being closed down en masse, when unfortunate monks were being thrown out of their monasteries, when thousands of priests and Orthodox laymen were appealing to you in prayer, with faces full of trust and hope—did you utter a single word in their defense ? Did you ever raise a finger to help them ?"

As he himself admits, Levitin is a passionate man and spares neither himself nor others. He was imprisoned in May, 1971, sentenced to three years in a penal camp; the accusation was based on his publishing activity.

A number of personalities, among them Y. Titov, wrote a letter to the World Council of Churches with the request for mediation, noting therein : [116]

> We believing Christians deeply mourn the fact that the Russian Orthodox Church finds her defenders among church members and the lower clergy and not among the bishops of the Russian Church, whose representatives in many ways are nothing else than unfruitful fig trees, completely submissive to the Council for Religious Affairs !

Besides the measures taken against institutional church life, there is also the anti-religious propaganda which greatly increased in this period and seriously threatened religious life within families. School children were enlisted to give information on what happened at home, and atheistic propagandists began to apply a more personal touch by instituting "family visiting." It has happened repeatedly that children were taken from parents to protect them from their religious fanaticism. It has also happened that Orthodox believers were treated against their will in psychiatric institutions because they were too much fascinated by religion. The cases of Yuri Titov and G. M. Shimanov, who gave detailed reports of their experiences, are described by M. Bourdeaux.[117]

Reports of the sharpened anti-religious measures have become well known everywhere in the last few years and have given rise among many in the West to the same question raised by both Levitin and the Moscow priests. Ought not the Russian hierarchy to have taken a more determined attitude in all this and have come to the defense of the personal rights of the believers and the

able that this question is asked. It is even a sign of courage when it is asked by Moscow priests and Orthodox believers. But it seems to me that we ask this question too easily and that we ought to ponder more deeply the situation of the church in Russia before we risk passing a negative judgment on the attitude of Russian church leaders. In a later section I shall return to this subject.

2. Church and Peace

In the extension of the discussion of the too cooperative attitude of the Russian church leaders in a period of oppression of church and religious life, we must examine the criticism of the active participation of the Russian church in the foreign policy of the U.S.S.R. This criticism became extremely vocal after the invasion of Czechoslovakia, an event which for many led to an ebbing away of sympathy and interest in the church in Russia.

During and after the war, after the Russian church again assumed a place in public life, a close co-operation developed between church and state, particularly in the area of foreign policy. Some are inclined to suggest that the church was enlisted for the benefit of Soviet political goals. In the establishment of Russian influence in the Middle East, church and state walked hand in hand. In May, 1945, after an interview with Stalin in April, Patriarch Alexi visited different cities in the Middle East (Teheran, Damascus, Beirut, Jerusalem, Cairo), an endeavor which naturally had great propaganda value. In addition, we must not forget that from ancient times the church had always attached great importance to the bonds uniting it with the other churches in that area and had always posed as the protector of Christians in the Arabic world. Within the framework of the annexation of new districts by the U.S.S.R., the church has also rendered important services. The church has played a great role in the Russification and Orthodoxing of those areas, as appears from the integration of the Uniate.

The church has also had an important place in the Russian "Peace Offensive." Since 1949 when the patriarch issued his summons to defend the peace, the church fought along with conviction. Metropolitan Nikolai (1891 - 1961) became one of the most prominent figures in the peace movement inspired by Moscow and has been one of the great Russian church personalities in the post-war years.[118] He defended the foreign policy of the Soviet Union with great conviction everywhere on foreign soil; perhaps he saw a possibility therein to strengthen the position of the church in Russia. In addition to this somewhat opportunistic motive, we must, in judging the matter, certainly reckon with a nationalistic motive. Nationalism is especially strong in Eastern Europe, and the war has greatly increased national patriotism among Russian church people, thereby linking them to a centuries-old tradition of church agreement with the politics of the state. Yet this very docility of the Russian church has led to a breach between the representatives of the churches in Eastern Europe and a number of their friends in the West, and to the disruption of the Prague Christian Peace Conference which has existed since 1958. This organization was founded on the initiative of J. Hromadka, H. Iwand, and others to bring about contact between Christians from Eastern and Western Europe, to combat the cold war mentality, and to influence the churches to devote themselves to the service of friendship, reconciliation, and peaceful co-operation among the nations.

The ecumenical agencies protested fiercely against the occupation of Czechoslovakia in August, 1968. Those who with a certain contempt speak of "striking up an acquaintance with the East" and accuse the World Council of Churches of one-sidedness in political utterances, ignore the sharp protests which the World Council of Churches then aimed at the leaders of the Eastern European churches, with the request that they choose their own position in the light of these events. Alexi's answer mirrors the official Russian point of view and rejects all protests.[119] That is the way it went also in the Prague Peace Movement. A recent publication, in which all documents of this movement from the period 1968 - 1971 are exhibited,[120] reveals how the Czech secretary-general Ondra had to resign due to political pressure and how every criticism of the Eastern bloc countries was smothered.

Hromadka retired as chairman "because our movement lost its sovereignty in believing and acting." Others also confirmed the fact that the outside pressure which made Hromadka resign and made it impossible to freely take a position on political questions, prevented criticism of Soviet policy (for example, in regard to Latin American countries or relations with China) and hindered Christian Marxist dialogue. The forty-two-year-old metropolitan Nikodim (civilian name Boris Rotov) assumed the leadership of the Prague Peace Movement after 1968 and maneuvered the whole cause — at the direction of the authorities—into the official line. At the last meeting in Prague, from September 30 to October 3, 1971, he was chosen the new president. But most of the participants and board members of the Peace Conference withdrew because, as the Englishman David Paton wrote to Nikodim: "It has become clear that the only basis whereon we can co-operate is the acceptance of the leading Eastern position." Metropolitan Nikodim has been severely criticized; for some he is no more than a tool of the state within the church. To this judgment we shall presently return.

3. *Wurmbrand and the Underground Church*

A third factor contributing to the growth of a negative frame of mind toward the Orthodox Church and its leaders is the appearance of Richard Wurmbrand, well known as a speaker at many meetings in America and Europe and as author of the book *The Underground Church, Martyred for Christ's Sake*.[121] Born in Bucharest (Rumania) in 1909, and active in missions among the Jews from 1939 to 1948, he represented the World Council of Churches in Rumania for some time after the war, carrying on relief work and illegal evangelism among Russian soldiers. In 1948 he was arrested on the street and experienced many years of exceedingly cruel and severe imprisonment. In 1956, after Stalin's death, he received amnesty, but because he so fiercely attacked the Communist Party—the Murderer's Gang—and because of his underground evangelistic activity, he was convicted again in 1959, this time for twenty-five years. Released in 1964, he was granted permission to leave the country in 1965 after the Norwegian Jewish Mission paid the state a ransom price for him.

Since then he has devoted himself to a fiercely anti-communist activity in the interest of what he calls the underground church in the Communist world. In an emotional, highly simplified way, filled with generalization, he speaks about the work of the Christian underground, attacking the "false leaders" of the church in both East and West. He sees himself as a leader of a secret mission work behind the Iron Curtain (p. 59) and stands ready to brand as traitors each one who maintains contact with the churches there. Consequently, he is a bitter opponent of the World Council and utters the wildest accusations against Western church leaders to the effect that they are not concerned about the martyrs but "together with the Russian Orthodox and Baptist leaders, dine sumptuously in the name of the imposing World Council of Churches, while the saints in prison eat cabbage that wasn't cleaned, as I have eaten it in the name of Jesus Christ" (p. 72). Though he is rather insinuating in his judgments, he finds a large and generous audience whenever he beats the anti-communist drum. "The West is asleep and must be awakened" (p. 78). Ministers and bishops in Eastern Europe are for him mere hired men of the regime, secret agents, informers on their church members. Churches that may be visited by foreigners are show churches, show windows where a religious freedom which doesn't exist is displayed. On the other hand, he paints a picture of the underground church as a strong ecclesiastical organization spread throughout the whole Communist world.

It is all very simplistic, and because of the absolute prejudice portrays a distorted picture. As far as he is concerned, Josef Hromadka is not a Christian and Metropolitan Nikodim of Leningrad is a secret agent, as is A. Karev, the secretary of the Russian Baptists. In the story of the Russian Evangelical Christians and Baptists I have cast a different light upon Karev and have tried to do more justice to the peculiarly difficult mission which church leaders have in Communist countries. It is also inaccurate to suggest that there exists in Eastern Europe a widespread, coherent underground church. The situation is different in each country. In Poland, Czechoslovakia, East Germany, and Hungary it is different than in Bulgaria, Rumania, or Russia. There is no question but that there are in Russia Christian groups that lead an illegal existence, unrecognized by the state. Some, like the separated Baptists (Initsiativniki), do not shun publicity. Because of their religion, a number of Initsiativniki were captured—a few hundred whose names are accurately known. Not much happens in the U.S.S.R. that doesn't become known beyond the borders. So when Wurmbrand speaks of tens of thousands, he is definitely in the wrong.

The American W. C. Fletcher published a book on the Russian Orthodox Church underground in which he describes a number of groups that lead an illegal existence,[122] of which the True Orthodox Church is the most widespread. Its adherents consider themselves the spiritual heirs of Patriarch Tikhon (1865 - 1925), chosen in 1917 as the first patriarch after the synodical period that had endured from the time of Peter the Great (1721). He is regarded by this group as the true representative of the church, refusing to bend before the Soviet regime, and they condemn the patriarchs Sergii and Alexi who, according to their way of thinking, concluded an unjust compromise with the state. This illegal Orthodox group, therefore, does indeed represent a political position conflicting with that of the regime. But this is not the case with every group. After a minute investigation, Fletcher determined that this underground Orthodox movement is of little consequence numerically.

Naturally, there is a variety of sectarian groups — typical Russian sects like there have always been in Russian history, such as the Dukhobors and Khlysty, but also Western groups such as Jehovah's Witnesses and Pentecostals. As under czarist rule, they were forced to lead an underground existence. Then there are many in Carpatho-Ukraine and in the district of Lvov who, after the annexation of their territory by the U.S.S.R., have not been able to accept the integration into Orthodoxy of their own church, with its ties to Rome, and who passively resist the Orthodox Church. Technically these churches (originating after the Union of Brest-Litovsk, 1595, and Ushgorod, 1646) are completely dissolved; yet in the old city of Lvov it appears that this integration was never really accepted. Very many listen to the Radio Vaticana broadcasts from Bishop Slipi who, after many years of imprisonment, took refuge in Rome in 1963. He was the successor to the famous metropolitan Count Szeptycki (deceased 1944). It is striking how much attention in the atheism museum in Lvov, sheltered in one of the many churches, is paid to this prince of the church who became a national symbol. He is placed in a very negative light—the whole museum, as a matter of fact, seems devoted to denigrating the Uniat Church. Certainly a sign that the authorities deem it necessary to combat the ever present longing among the people for their own church historically united with Rome.

Another observation is that boundaries between legal and illegal church activity in Russia are difficult to draw. Especially in the last sixty years, because of the measures which the government took against the churches, many people were driven into the catacombs. By this somewhat emotional expression we mean that they were forced to practice their church life in an illegal manner. The forced closing of churches meant, after all, that in most cases public worship did not stop but that it was resumed in private homes, which was forbidden and hence constituted a violation of Soviet law. The same can be said of the closing of monasteries. (In 1957 there were about 20,000 churches, in 1960 about 11,500; the number of monasteries shrunk from 67 to 32, the number of in-service priests from 30,000 to 14,000). The prohibition against the religious influencing of the young and the restrictions on the baptism of children are bringing many to resort to that twilight zone of religious activities not officially permitted. The often tremendous distance to the nearest church and the scarcity of priests are bringing believers to resort to having their children baptized by illegally operating ministers and taking part in meetings that are outside the framework of the law.

People who want to be loyal to the regime are brought by that very regime to illegal dealings and an "underground" religiosity. Thus an estrangement from Soviet society is promoted. The church as such is a marginal group in Russia and it doesn't take much to make it take up an existence outside the boundaries of the officially sanctioned. The state recognizes this condition with some apprehension. It is precisely those government circles which consider a strict control and a firm grip on church life a necessity that are thereby moved to adopt a certain amount of moderation in the application of anti-religious measures. Some of the more accommodating measures taken with the official churches can certainly be explained as the concern not to drive too many believers into illegal currents and groups where control would be far more difficult.

Then there is still an entirely different "underground church" in Russia, though this name would be barely understood by the people themselves. As A. E. Levitin writes in his 1970 letter to Pope Paul VI, published in the West, the modern Russian youth is a restless, seeking youth and many boys and girls are experiencing a religious breakthrough.[123] He writes of a young engineer who had sought contact with a believing neighbor lady. She brought him in contact with someone who was better grounded

173

theologically than she, and there followed a number of serious and systematic conversations. After two months the engineer said to his wife, "You know, after long deliberation, I have decided to receive baptism." His young wife answered, "I was baptized a week ago, and I have also had our child baptized." He mentions more examples, confirmed by other sources, that particularly among the young, absolutely loyal intelligentsia there is a strong interest in religion. It is difficult for them to come into the open about this, since they do not wish to undermine their social positions. They attend church where they cannot be recognized. There is an interest in church music and iconology, and they plead for the preservation of old churches.

Often these young people do not feel at home in these church services — a strange world, a hard-to-understand Church Slavonic liturgy — and they do not know how to conduct themselves. Faithful church members who have withstood the storms of the times and look upon the church as part of themselves, the traditional old people, are not often very open and hospitable toward the hesitantly entering young seekers. This is somewhat understandable if one remembers how much trouble these young Communists have given believers, as Alexander Solzhenitsyn's story "The Easter Procession" tells us. Many experience what my sixteen-year-old son did when some time ago he attended a divine service in the cathedral in Lvov. Attentive and deeply moved by this first experience of the beauty and solemnity of an Orthodox Church service, he was thrown into confusion by an old lady rapping him on the knuckles and grumbling in an unfriendly way because he was standing with his hands behind his back. As others have assured me, those who remain faithful church-goers are not always equally openhearted to young people who come once, who are seeking, but often do not know what.

Levitin in his letter to the Pope designates as one of the tasks confronting the Russian Orthodox Church the reformation of the liturgy. The young no longer understand the forms and usages that have grown up in the course of the centuries and the religious youth seldom visit the churches. They are attracted by the works of N. Berdyaev and S. N. Bulgakov, they read stenciled articles, and gather around a priest or minister, but they are not drawn to the church service in its present form. That may be the case for some, but others are attracted precisely by the liturgy. There are examples of young university men who, when in a strange church where they could not be recognized, spontaneously joined the choir, singing what was not exactly easy church music. The "silent" believers sometimes suddenly step into the open. A remarkable event is described as taking place in the Moscow State Theater[124] where an anti-religious play was to be presented with Alexander Rostovtsev taking the leading role. It was a tasteless piece: in the play an altar cross was fashioned from beer and vodka bottles, priests danced around it and nuns sat drinking vodka and spewing forth blasphemous words. Then comes Rostovtsev with a Bible in his hand. The idea is that he is to read two verses from the Sermon on the Mount (from Matthew), then hurl the book away and join the dissolute party. But he reads on slowly: "Blessed are they that mourn." He is silent for a moment and the public notices that something is happening outside the script. It is quiet in the theater. After a slight pause he reads on: "Blessed are they that hunger and thirst after righteousness ... Blessed are they that are persecuted ..." So he continues until the end of the chapter. No one remonstrates. Then he crosses himself and exclaims: "Lord, remember me when thou comest in thy kingdom."

After this premiere the play is no longer presented and the name of Rostovtsev is no longer mentioned.

There are witnesses of Christ, there is a church out-side of the church, also in Russia. A foreign visitor asked a priest in Zagorsk if there really was an underground church in Russia next to and over against the official church. "An underground church," he said, "what do you call an underground church? The underground church has many storeys. The more you look up, the smaller they get. On the top storey, way above the ground and visible to all, stands but one man [he meant the patriarch]. Everyone sees him, everyone sees what he is doing, but no one can see his feet, for they are hidden."(125) But when one is speaking about religious currents in Russia, one will have to rid himself of the idea that a sort of anti-communistic underground exists, the idea that Wurmbrand conveys. There is no question about this, except perhaps of a few small groups of Tikhonites. Even the separatist Baptists express themselves openly as being supporters of the regime, opposing only the meddling of the state in the affairs of the church and the restrictive regulations in regard to religion. And Levitin, best-known representative of the Orthodox opposition, writes:

> To the question, what do the Russian youth want? one can answer in a few words: they want a socialistic democracy ... the only possible reality of the coming century. Our people do not want capitalism ... at the same time, the Russian people and especially the youth reject Stalinism and Maoism in all their expressions and variants. Russia wants complete freedom of expression and scientific research, freedom of religious and philosophic conviction. Economy without private ownership and full freedom of expression—that is social democracy.

Speaking of an "underground church" as Wurmbrand does, suggesting that it is a "beautiful secret organization," evokes a wrong image. By placing this talk in an emotional

176

anti-communist context he brings harm to the believers in the Communist world. There is no organized underground church. There are the seekers and there are the quiet, simple folk; there are groups on or over the edge of what is legally permissible, and there are non-registered Baptist groups who continually strive to get recognition, and there are many sectarians of which some, such as the "Silent" and the "Wanderers," are completely estranged from society.

There are also priests and believers in the church who oppose the church leadership. Levitin speaks of an authority crisis in the church that arises from the fact that bishops as well as the patriarch have lost their authority among the believers. According to many they went too far in their compromise with the state; they showed themselves too docile.

Wurmbrand cannot be considered the representative of all these groups and currents. In many ways he compromises them by his twisted picture of the political reality and by his mass campaigns. Contacts with Eastern European churches are possible on a variety of levels. Brother Andrew[126] tells some absorbing tales of his experiences as a "Bible smuggler." He is less pretentious and less politically motivated than Wurmbrand, more a real colporteur and evangelist. He does not fulminate against the official churches and leaves room for other forms of contact with Eastern European churches. Wurmbrand is no trustworthy source of information and causes much damage. Good and sober information is necessary, for a well-informed public opinion can certainly have a calming influence and can ease the pressure on some believers.

Even though one is critical of some of the public actions and pronouncements of the Russian hierarchs, one ought to guard oneself against attacking a church struggling to remain in existence, a church that in the last fifty years has produced more martyrs for the faith than any other in the world.

Between Loyalty and Martyrdom

It is indeed very shortsighted to presuppose that Russian church leaders never raised their voice against the actions taken by the Soviet authorities. We need not go back to the time of Patriarch Tikhon, nor to the many martyrs who died in distant camps, to know that there have been courageous witnesses of the faith. In the biography of the present patriarch as presented in the *Journal of the Moscow Patriarchate,* nothing is told of his work over a period of thirty some years. The custom is to pass over the years of imprisonment and exile without a word.

Nor may one presuppose that someone who entered a monastery in 1927, during a time of grave persecution, was an opportunist and chose the way of easy adjustment.

> Many bishops have fought and protested the injustice done to the church, and have lost. Many capitulated only when they saw that the damage done by their public protest was greater than when they remained silent and endured. Moreover, not only did they themselves often have to suffer for their courageous words, but their followers as well. Since the beginning of the persecution by the Communists, the hierarchs of the Russian Orthodox Church saw themselves faced with the same dilemma: to protest and thereby risk more serious reprisals, or keep silent and earn the insults of their persecutors and the scorn of their believing followers. What can best serve the church in the given situation and where lies the lesser evil ? A real question of conscience ! [127]

A clear example of what is said here can be seen in the behavior of Patriarch Alexi in December, 1959, when the pressure of the state on the church was increased. During the visit of a delegation from the World Council of Churches in Moscow under the leadership of Dr. W. A. Visser 't Hooft, there appeared in *Pravda* an extremely offensive and provocative article written by the archpriest and professor A. Osipov. An unexpected sharp reaction followed, for the church deprived him and others "who publicly had blasphemed the name of God" of their offices and thrust them out of its fellowship. The church historian Chrysostom calls this "an heroic act," the more so since the resolution was also published. In addition the patriarch spoke publicly at a meeting of the peace movement held in January, 1960, about the virtues of the church and its oneness with the people and observed that despite this fact "it had to endure attacks and slander." It was a public though carefully worded protest against the new measures of the state. The effect was not slow in coming, not a lessening of the pressure but a heightening. Metropolitan Nikolai was stripped of his functions and disappeared from public life until the news came of his unexpected death, December 13, 1961. The people of Moscow took for granted that he was murdered. Even Nikolai, the man of the Soviet peace movement and leader of the church's foreign relations, a virulent defender of the regime, was not spared a martyr's death. Chrysostom, the Catholic historian who fled Russia after the war, says in this connection: "From the change in his attitude (it was he who had effected Osipov's deposition) one can see that his behavior did not proceed from an unprincipled opportunism but grew out of his concern for the church. When he noticed that the government still strove after the liquidation of the church, he wanted no part of it. As long as the government was ready to tolerate the church and sometimes to help her, he exerted himself not to antagonize it." Nikolai provides an instructive example for each one who from his Western situation judges that the Russian church ought to protest more.

By order of the authorities, an important change in the position of priests in the congregation was brought about by the Synod of Bishops in 1961. All financial and economic arrangements were taken from them and placed in the hands of the church members, the so-called "Twenty," the minimum number of Soviet citizens necessary for registration as a congregation. According to Soviet law, church buildings and religious articles (all belonging to the state) can be loaned for use to citizens belonging to that religion and who assume responsibility for their upkeep. The government made the bishops aware of this and they withdrew from the priests the responsibility for the upkeep of the church. From our point of view this seems a sound measure, but this ruling opened new possibilities for the government to get a grip on the internal life of the church. It has happened that clearly anti-religious persons penetrated the board of the "Twenty" in order to undermine congregational life from the inside out. In the report to the Synod (1971), Pimen indeed subtly hints at this when he says, "Sometimes laymen who have caused unrest in their congregations fail to approach their pastors with fitting respect."[128]

We must not forget that the church in Russia is a tolerated church, to whom the omnipotent state has left but a very small space. On the other side, the constitution guarantees freedom for the church. In 1968, Kuroyedov, chairman of the Council for Religious Affairs in the cabinet council of the U.S.S.R., paraphrased this freedom thus: "The church with us is free and independent in the fulfillment of its only function—to satisfy the religious need of the believers. But forbidden are the religious influencing of minors, meetings and religious activities outside the church, religious meetings for children, charity, relief funds, church cultural institutions, hospitals, sports associations, and the like."

180

Thus the church lives in a ghetto, and on the basis of this concept of freedom one can easily find a way to condemn someone for transgressing the Soviet law. When one gathers in a home or in a woods because the congregation has not been registered, or conducts a children's Sunday School, one is condemned—not, naturally, for religious reasons, but for overstepping the law! Persecution of the faith will always be publicly denied by the official spokesmen. It makes no sense at all, therefore, to ask a bishop, for example, about it in an interview. He will never be able to do anything but say that there is freedom for the church and that one is not persecuted for one's faith, and that one must naturally obey the laws of the state. He will admit that people are condemned because they break the law, but not because of their faith. We must not, therefore, pose such questions, if the purpose of the interview is to become informed and not to embarrass people and tempt them to make statements which could have serious consequences for themselves and the church. Russian bishops who appear abroad are shackled people. When it comes to these things, there is no greater Soviet conformist than Metropolitan Nikodim of Leningrad, head of the Department for Foreign Relations of the Russian Orthodox Church. But what he does in secret, within the possibilities he has through contact with the government, for churches and individual believers who are in difficulties can never become known.

Alongside the very limited, constitutionally guaranteed freedom to conduct church services, there is the other factor, namely the anti-religious propaganda carried on by the government and the official party agencies (the difference between the two is only theoretical). The Marxist state is consciously out to eliminate all religion with whatever means it has at its disposal. To the extent that this has not yet been realized and the churches are still tolerated, that is due to the difficulties the official agencies experience in exterminating religion. The anti-religious activity has only a limited success. The following conversation is illustrative : "Thank God," said the farmer's wife, "it's going to rain." "But comrade," said the head of the collective farm, "you know very well that, thank God, God doesn't exist." "Naturally, comrade, but what if, God forbid, He did exist ?"

I have already mentioned the search among many young people, especially from intellectual circles, for a living religion. Someone has concluded: [129] "Marxism-Leninism in Russia is petrified and has ceased even to exert a quasi-religious attractive power on the people. But what will fill the vacuum created by the dying of an ideology ?" The church has a task in regard to people molded by dialectical materialism and Russian nationalism. An overwhelming task for which theologically it is hardly equipped and still has little opportunity. Yet that is its essential mandate for which it must arm itself, even if for the moment it can do no more than try to continue to exist as an organism—the only one in the U.S.S.R.—that has its roots in soil other than the official monopolistic ideology.

But observations about the failure of this state ideology to truly reach man do not permit us to close our eyes to the fact that an aggressive atheism is united with a state which internally wields absolute power. Since 1918 the church has wrestled with the problem of its relationship to this state. Determinative for the attitude of the Orthodox Church has been the declaration of Metropolitan Sergii (later, in 1943, chosen as patriarch) given in July, 1927.

In his Declaration of Loyalty to the Soviet government, he explains, among other things:

> We want to be Orthodox and at the same time we want to accept the Soviet Union as our earthly fatherland and to be citizens of the Union

"not only for wrath, but also for conscience's sake" (Rom. 13:5) ... only world-estranged dreamers can imagine that so great a fellowship as the Orthodox Church can hide itself from the state and so exist in the state. Now that our church is firmly resolved and without hesitation treads the way of loyalty, those people will have to behave themselves differently, leave their political sympathies at home, and carry only their faith into the church, working together with us in that faith ... only the relationship to the powers that be is changed, the faith and the Orthodox life remain untouched.

Metropolitan Sergii introduced a new era in the relationship of church and state. His Declaration of Loyalty was strongly criticized in those years, especially among emigrant circles. But Chrysostom[130] writes this about it:

One may not speak too lightly of the invincibility of the church; this promise refers to the whole church and never to the church in a certain country. The once mighty patriarchates of Alexandria and Antioch are now almost without significance, lonely islands in an Islamic sea. The same fate might have struck the Russian church; instead, the number of believers is now estimated at forty or even fifty million. Numerically, it is and always has been the strongest church in Orthodoxy. The Russian church had to tread a long, particularly difficult way in the time between the death of Patriarch Tikhon and the Second World War, a way fraught with bitter suffering, scorn, and unbelievable humiliation. That it—at least for the present—has survived this time of terror is inconceivable apart from the person of the metropolitan, later patriarch, Sergii.

As some have said, the church has made use of camouflage, yet it remained the church of Christ. Beaten, doomed to silence and to suffering, sometimes apparently dancing to the whims of a hostile regime, it was and is in its very being an offense to the powers that be and a sign of that Kingdom which is in the world but not of it, a thorn in the flesh of a totalitarian ideology. It has accepted the political and social reality wherein it is living. It tries to find room in it to fulfill its mandate as it sees it, and if possible, to build for the welfare of the people. Loyalty to the state is naturally also a compromise with the state. Some upbraid the heads of the church for going too far. Undoubtedly, imprudent mistakes were made, but we must be careful about measuring by our standards. For an atomic scientist like A. D. Sakharov to take a stand, in a politically adroit way, for the rights of minority groups and the persecuted is quite different than for a church leader to try the same thing. Sakharov belongs to the most privileged and honored group of intellectuals. It is unthinkable that, for example, Nikodim could protest openly and be allowed to continue his work. But his silence does not mean that he agrees with everything that happens or, as some maintain, that he himself is directly responsible. We must not confuse the persecuted with the persecutors. Naturally one can be critical of his position, particularly in the realm of international politics, just as one could be critical of the political position of Billy Graham in his relation to Nixon. One must then also consider that Graham did not have to act the way he did while Nikodim cannot act otherwise; thus he obtains a freedom to participate in world ecumenism which otherwise he would never have. His pronouncements we must test critically, but we may not brush him off as a secret agent of Communism. He is a man of the church, who consciously wants the isolated Russian church to play a role in ecumenism. He is definitely interested in theological conversations, such as those carried on between the Russian church and the Evangelical Church in Germany, and pleads that they may continue regularly. He has built up a new relationship with the Roman Catholic Church, and he promotes contact between Orthodox and Oriental churches. He graduated in 1970 with a doctoral dissertation on Pope John XXIII, and has gathered a group of young, gifted theologians around him. He seems receptive to bringing renewal to many areas of the church, a very delicate task particularly in the Russian Orthodox Church. He has pleaded that fellowship with the Old Believers be restored, as it actually was at the last synod. (The Raskol, secession, originated 300 years ago when Patriarch Nikon pushed through certain liturgical reforms). In the conversations with the Old Believers, he also made a plea for their involvement in the political peace movement. One could say: "See, here once again is Soviet politics." It is better to proceed from the idea that in Russia what the church wants had better be translated into concepts that are acceptable to the government; thus, when ecclesiastical fellowship between the Orthodox and the Old Believers is to be restored, that is promoting the peace movement.

We are not dealing here with a bishop's apology. We are concerned with a good understanding of the place of the church in a Communist country. The much-criticized sons of Orthodoxy are driven by a sincere care for the life and working of their church.

It is very difficult for us to pass judgment on their position. Critical voices from their own church penetrate to us. This opposition is important, for it can protect the official church from going too far in harmony with the authorities and reverting back to a state-church attitude like in the old days. Somewhere there is a point at which the *non possumus* (further we cannot go) is spoken. Nikolai and Levitin (and innumerable others) have known it. But this is at the same time the point where loyalty

185

turns into martyrdom. Therefore we are called upon to exercise restraint in our judgment. Who are we to challenge the brothers to become martyrs ?

The best contribution we can make is to show how a church motivated by the Gospel can act critically, prophetically, as a guidance-giving movement in the political and social happenings of today. In the non-Communist world the church has ample freedom for this. How we use that freedom is a question for us to answer.

Notes

(1) W. Birnbaum, *Christenheit in Sowjet-Russland*, Tübingen 1961, p. 45.

(2) Z. R. Dittrich, *Het verleden van Oost-Europa*, Zeist 1963.

(3) A. M. Amman, *Abrisz der Ostslavischen Kirchengeschichte*, Vienna 1950, pp. 14 ff.; R. Stupperich, "Die Kirche des alten Russland in ihren nationalen Eigenart," *Kirche im Osten* 11 (1968) 20.

(4) R. Wittram, *Baltische Kirchengeschichte*, Göttingen 1956.

(5) P. Amburger, *Geschichte des Protestantismus in Russland*, Stuttgart 1961, p. 16.

(6) R. Stupperich, "Geschichtliche Wandlungen und Lebensbedingungen des slavischen Protestantismus," *Kirche im Osten* 2 (1959) 80.

(7) I. Smolitsch, *Geschichte der Russischen Kirche 1700-1917*, Leiden 1964, p. 65.

(8) H. Dalton, *Urkundenbuch der evangelisch-reformierten Kirche in Russland*, Gotha 1889, pp. 21-23.

(9) H. Dalton, *Geschichte der Reformierten Kirche in Russland*, Gotha 1865, p. 197.

(10) W. Kahle, *Aufsätze zur Entwicklung der evangelischen Gemeinden in Russland*, Leiden 1962, p. 3.

(11) W. Kahle, "Der Protestantismus in Russland und in der Sawjet-union," *Zeitschrift für Religions- und Geistesgeschichte* Vol. XXI (1969) 335.

(12) Dalton, *Geschichte*, p. 202.

(13) *Ibid.*, p. 213.

(14) Kahle, *Aufsätze*, p. 14.

(15) R. Stupperich, *Kirchenordnungen der Evangelisch-Lutherischen Kirche in Russland*, Ulm 1959, p. 171.

(16) J. Hosmar, *De Vriezenveense handel op Rusland, zijn begin, uitbreiding en betekenis.* Jaarboek Twente 1965.

(17) J. Scheltema, *Rusland en de Nederlanden, beschouwd in derzelver wederkerige betrekkingen,* Amsterdam 1817, 4 volumes, vol. 1, p. 20.

(18) *Ibid.*, p. 363.

(19) H. Dalton, *Geschichte,* p. 113.

(20) L. Knappert, *Schets van eene geschiedenis onzer Handelskerken I, Nederlands Archief van Kerkgeschiedenis* XXI (1928).

(21) Scheltema, *Rusland,* part 4, p. 332.

(22) *Ibid.*, part 3, p. 113.

(23) *De Ned. Hervormde Gemeente in Petersburg 1717-1898,* n.d., n.p. According to Knappert, the writer is B. Cruys from Petersburg. Included in the book are the Rules of Order of the Netherlands Reformed Church in St. Petersburg from 1875 and a directory of the members of the consistory.

(24) L. Knappert, E. A. J. Tamling, minister of the Netherlands Reformed Church in St. Petersburg, *Nederlands Archief voor Kerkgeschiedenis* XVIII (1936) 21; W. Kahle, "Die St. Petersburger Briefe des reformierten Pastors E. A. J. Tamling," *Kyrios* 3 (1963) 129.

(25) Kahle, *Aufsätze*, p. 11.

(26) Abel Hermant, *Madame de Krüdener: L'amie du tzar Alexander I, 1764-1824,* Paris 1934. E. J. Knapton, *The Lady of the Holy Alliance: The Life of Julie de Krüdener,* New York 1939.

(27) Edition of 1878 with Foreword by Parisot.

(28) W. Gutsche, *Westliche Quellen des russischen Stundismus,* Kassel 1956, p. 23.

(29) Werner Krause, "Die Bibel in Russland," *Kirche im Osten* 1 (1958) 16.

(30) E. Benz, *Die abendländische Sendung der östlich-orthodoxen Kirche,* Wiesbaden 1950.

(31) Kahle, *Aufsätze*, p. 137.

(32) L. Müller, *Der Einfluss des Protestantismus auf das orthodoxe Kirchen- und Geistesleben in Russland, Evangelisches und orthodoxes Christentum in Begegnung und Auseinandersetzung,* Hamburg 1952, p. 168.

(33) Krause, *Die Bibel,* p. 17; R. A. Klostermann, *Probleme der Ostkirche,* p. 361.

(34) Michael Klimenko, *Anfänge des Baptismus in Südrussland [Ukraine] nach offiziellen Dokumenten,* Erlangen 1957, p. 22.

188

(35) Klostermann, *Probleme*, p. 59.
(36) Klimenko, *Anfänge*, p. 80.
(37) Klostermann, *Probleme*, p. 384.
(38) Klimenko, *Anfänge*, p. 43.
(39) W. Gutsche, *Westliche Quellen*, p. 57.
(40) Klimenko, *Anfänge*, p. 82.
(41) *Westliche Quellen*, p. 78.
(42) W. B. Edgerton, *Leskov, Paskov, the Stundists, and a Newly Discovered Letter*, Orbis Scriptus, München 1966, pp. 187-199.
(43) Fürstin Sophie Lieven, *Eine Saat die reiche Frucht brachte*, Basel 1952, p. 14.
(44) Gutsche, *Westliche Quellen*, p. 81.
(45) R. Stupperich, "Geschichtliche Wandlungen und Lebensbedingungen des slavischen Protestantismus," *Kirche im Osten* 2 (1959) 94.
(46) Nicolaï Arseniev, *La Sainte Moscou, Tableau de la vie religieuse et intellectuelle russe au XIXe siècle*, Paris, p. 34.
(47) Kahle, *Aufsätze*, p. 89.
(48) W. Kolarz, *Religion in the Soviet Union*, London 1961.
(49) Constantin de Grunwald, *La vie religieuse en URSS*, Paris 1961.
(50) E. Benz, *Die russische Kirche und das abendländische Christentum*, Nymphenburger Verlagshandlung 1966, pp. 153-173.
(51) *Probleme*, p. 218.
(52) Smolitsch, *Geschichte der Russischen Kirche 1700-1917*, p. 88.
(53) *Kirche im Osten* 1 (1958) 14; Klostermann, *Probleme*, p. 235.
(54) R. Stupperich, "Russische Sekten," *RGG* V. p. 1232.
(55) Serge Bolshakoff, *Russian Nonconformity. The Story of "Unofficial" Religion in Russia*, Philadelphia n.d., p. 115.
(56) Dittrich, *Her verleden von Oost-Europa*, p. 250.
(57) *Vestnik Spasenia—Heilsbode* 1967/3, cited by W. Kahle, "Kampf und Leiden," *Berliner Informationen*, April 1969.
(58) Kolarz, *Religion*, p. 288.
(59) I. S. Prochanov, *Erfolge des Evangeliums in Russland*, Wernigerode 1929.
(60) *Abrisz der Ostslavischen Kirchengeschichte*, p. 1610.
(61) Boleslav Szcesnick, *The Russian Revolution. A Collection of Documents*, Notre Dame University Press 1959.
(62) *Christenheit in Sowjet-Russland*, p. 159.
(63) Nikita Struve, *Christians in Contemporary Russia*, London 1967, p. 378; R. Stupperich, *Kirche und Staat. Gesetze und Verordnungen*, Witten 1962, p. 13.

189

(64) J. S. Curtiss, *The Russian Church and the Soviet State 1917-1950*, German translation, Munich 1957, p. 218.

(65) "Die Evangelisch-Lutherische Kirche in der Sovjet-Union 1917-1937." *Kirche im Osten* 2 (1959). H. Maurer.

(66) Kolarz, *Religion*, p. 298.

(67) Bolshakoff, *Russian Nonconformity*, p. 120.

(68) Michael Bourdeaux, *Religious Ferment in Russia: Protestant Opposition to Soviet Religious Policy*, London 1968, p. 55.

(69) *Ibid.*, p. 5.

(70) *Vosprosy filosofii* no. 3, 1941, cited by W. C. Fletcher/ A. J. Strover, *Religion and the Search for New Ideals in the USSR*, New York 1967, p. 79.

(71) M. Bourdeaux, *Opium of the People: The Christian Religion in the USSR*, London 1965, p. 159.

(72) *Dein Reich komme*, Mitteilungen vom Missionsbund Licht im Osten, September 1969, p. 68.

(73) Kahle, *Der Protestantismus in Russland*, p. 345.

(74) Bolshakoff, *Russian Nonconformity*, pp. 125-127.

(75) W. Kahle, "Fragen der Einheit im Bunde der Evangeliumchristen/Baptisten in der Sowjetunion," *Kyrios* 8 (1968) 164-179.

(76) W. Fletcher, "Protestant Influences on the Soviet Citizen," in *Religion and the Search for New Ideals*.

(77) Kahle, *Fragen der Einheit*, p. 177.

(78) B. Geissler/G. Stökl, *In Oriente Crux. Versuch einer Geschichte der reformatorischen Kirchen im Raum zwischen der Ostsee und dem Schwarzen Meer*, Stuttgart 1963, p. 424.

(79) Kolarz, *Religion in the Soviet Union*, p. 269.

(80) H. Roemmich, "Evangelische Gemeinden in Russland nach einem halben Jahrhundert Sovjetherrschaft," *Kirche im Osten* 14 (1971) 135-162. *Dein Reich komme*, March 1970, p. 13.

(81) Kahle, *Fragen der Einheit*, p. 178.

(82) Fletcher, "Protestant Influences on the Soviet Citizen," p. 76.

(83) *Kirche im Osten* 6 (1963) 135.

(84) Struve, *Christians in Contemporary Russia*, p. 293.

(85) B. R. Bociurkiw, "Church-State Relations in the USSR," *Survey, A Journal of Soviet and East European Studies*, January 1968, p. 24. Also published in M. Hayward/ W. C. Fletcher, *Religion and the Soviet State: A Dilemma of Power*, London 1969.

(86) Bourdeaux, *Opium of the People*, p. 217.

(87) Bourdeaux, *Religious Ferment*, p. 17.

(88) J. C. Pollock, *The Christians from Siberia*, London 1964. In German translation: *Und das Volk weinte die ganze Nacht*, Konstanz 1966; *Gott hinter Gittern*, Konstanz 1969.

(89) Herder correspondence August 1970, no. 8: *Die Reformbaptisten in der Sowjetunion*.

(90) *Nauka i Religia*, no. 9, 1966. *Science and Religion*, publication of the All-Union Association for the Dissemination of Scientific and Political Knowledge. This association was begun in 1947, replacing the League of Militant Atheists. The publication has appeared since 1959. Quoted from Bordeaux, *Religious Ferment*, p. 25.

(91) Bourdeaux, *Religious Ferment*, p. 20.

(92) Fletcher/Strover, *Religion and the Search for New Ideals*, p. 69.

(93) Bourdeaux, *Religious Ferment*, p. 36; W. Kahle, "Kampf und Leiden," *Berliner Informationen*, April 1969, Osteuropa.

(94) M. Bourdeaux and Peter Reddaway, "Church and State and Schism: Soviet-Baptist Today," in *Survey, A Journal of Soviet and East European Studies*, January 1968, pp. 48-66.

(95) W. Kahle, "Zu den Auseinandersetzungen und Spannungen unter den Evangelium-christen/Baptisten in der Sowjetunion," in *Berliner Informationen* jrg. 2/III, 1968, Osteuropa.

(96) *Kirche im Osten* 11 (1968) 135.

(97) *Dein Reich komme*, March 1970, p. 13.

(98) Adolf Klaupiks, *Baptist World Alliance News*, 12 January 1968. *Congressbook: Documents of Moscow 1966*, All-Union Conference of Evangelical Christian-Baptists.

(99) *The New York Times*, 29-7-1966.

(100) Struve, *Christians in Contemporary Russia*, p. 327.

(101) November 29, 1963, cited by Struve.

(102) Fletcher, "Protestant Influences on the Soviet Citizen," p. 65.

(103) Struve, *Christians in Contemporary Russia*, p. 627.

(104) *Dein Reich komme*, May.

(105) Herder correspondence, 24 August, 1970. *Congressbook: Proceedings of the All-Union Congress of Evangelical Christians-Baptists* 1969.

(106) *Dein Reich komme*, July 1970, pp. 4 and 10.

(107) *Handelsblad* 17 November 1969, *Dein Reich komme*, January 1970.

(108) *N.R.C.* 11 August 1970.

(109) Bourdeaux, *Religious Ferment*, p. 28.
(110) Bociurkiw, "Church-State Relations in the USSR," *Survey, A Journal of Soviet and East European Studies*, January 1968, p. 5.
(111) Kolarz, *Religion in the Soviet Union*, p. 258.
(112) Bociurkiw, "Church-State Relations in the USSR," p. 5.
(113) Wetter, *Survey*, p. 1.
(114) Struve, *Christians in Contemporary Russia*, pp. 404, 351. After the present manuscript was completed, there appeared M. Bourdeaux, *Faith on Trial in Russia*, London 1971.
(115) M. Bourdeaux, *Patriarch and Prophets: Persecution of the Russian Orthodox Church Today*, London 1969, p. 277. Also a number of documents of ecclesiastical opposition published in André Martin, *Les Croyants en URSS*, Paris 1970. See too the unusually objective book written by G. Simon, *Die Kirchen in Russland Berichte, Documente*, Munich 1971.
(116) N. Theodorowitsch, *Religion und Atheismus in der UdSSR*, Munich 1970, pp. 169, 49, 63, 69, 54.
(117) *The Church Times*, 1 October 1971, p. 6.
(118) J. Chrysostom, *Kirchengeschichte Russlands der neuesten Zeit*, vol. I, Munich 1965, vol. II, 1966, vol. III, 1968, pp. 128ff., 150ff., 225.
(119) Theodorowitsch, *Religion und Atheismus*, pp. 265 ff.
(120) *Christliche Friedens-Konferenz 1968-1971: Dokumente und Berichte*, Wuppertal 1971.
(121) *De Banier*, Vianen, n.d.
(122) W. C. Fletcher, *The Russian Orthodox Church Underground 1917-1970*, London 1971.
(123) Theodorowitsch, *Religion und Atheismus*, pp. 246ff.
(124) *Orthodoxe Rundschau* 1971—11, p. 19.
(125) *Sobornost* 1971—3, p. 194.
(126) *God's Smuggler*. Brother Andrew with John and Elisabeth Sherrill, London 1967.
(127) R. Hotz in *Die Hierarchie des Moskauer Patriarchats unter Beschuss- Orientierung*, Zürich 1971—7, p. 74.
(128) *Stimmen der Orthodoxie* 1971—10, p. 14.
(129) Max Hayward in Fletcher-Strover, *Religion and the Search for New Ideals in the USSR*, London 1965, p. 133.
(130) *Kirchengeschichte Russlands*, p. 67.